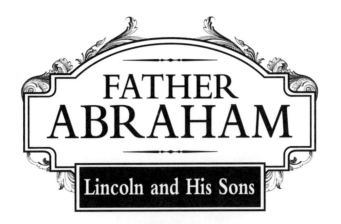

FATHER ABRAHAM

Lincoln and His Sons

Harold Holzer

CALKINS CREEK

Honesdale, Pennsylvania

Text copyright © 2011 by Harold Holzer
All rights reserved
Printed in the United States of America
Designed by Jeff George
First edition

ISBN: 978-1-59078-303-0

Library of Congress Control Number: 2010929520

Front jacket (left): Abraham Lincoln, photographed by
Anthony Berger of the Mathew Brady Studio in 1864;
(right, top to bottom): Robert, Willie, and Tad Lincoln.
Back jacket: Abraham Lincoln as he looked in 1860, the year
of his election as president. No one knows who took this
photograph, but it was probably made at the request of an artist
named Leonard Wells Volk, who used it as the model for a
statuette of the Republican candidate.

CALKINS CREEK
An Imprint of Boyds Mills Press, Inc.
815 Church Street
Honesdale, Pennsylvania 18431

10 9 8 7 6 5 4 3 2 1

To Remy and Adam's son, Charlie

—From Papa

"I regret the necessity of saying I have no daughters. I have three sons. . . .
They, with their mother, constitute my whole family."

ABRAHAM LINCOLN

October 19, 1860

CONTENTS

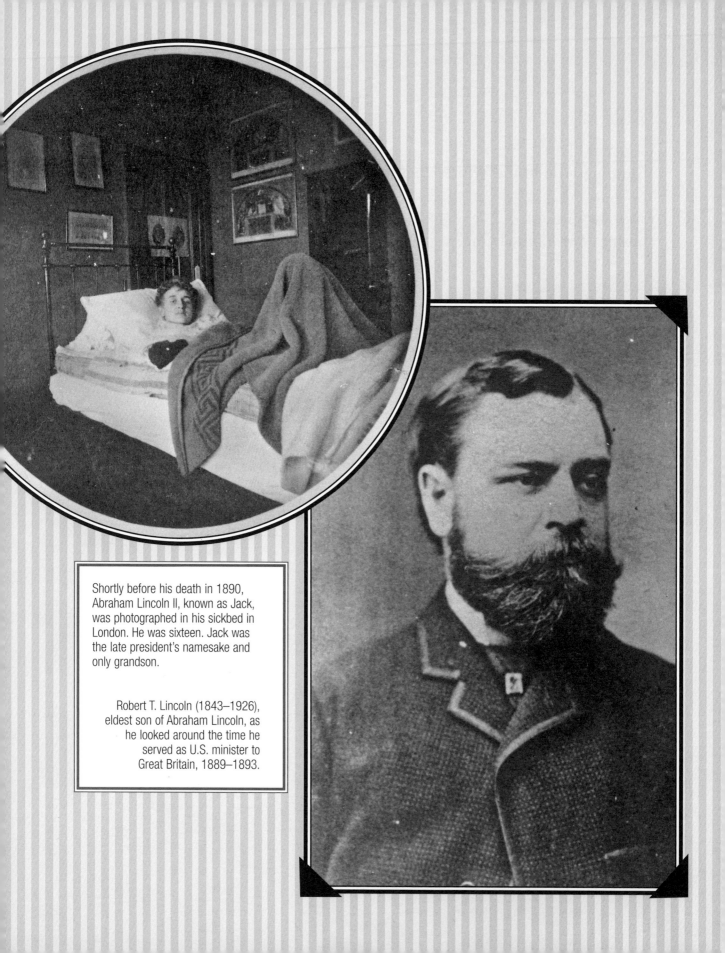

Shortly before his death in 1890, Abraham Lincoln II, known as Jack, was photographed in his sickbed in London. He was sixteen. Jack was the late president's namesake and only grandson.

Robert T. Lincoln (1843–1926), eldest son of Abraham Lincoln, as he looked around the time he served as U.S. minister to Great Britain, 1889–1893.

INTRODUCTION
Too Young, Too Soon

On a chill winter day in London, inside a darkened room at the American minister's beautiful home, a once healthy teenage boy lay on his deathbed. The best doctors in Europe had treated him. But they had done him more harm than good.

Surgery to lance a carbuncle—a painful skin infection—had left the young man feverish and weak. His wound grew worse and worse, and he developed blood poisoning. For a time, back around Christmas, he seemed to rally. His anxious mother and father prayed that he was on the road to recovery. But in the weeks that followed, he took a turn for the worse. The doctors could do no more. Little by little, the life flickered out of the boy's eyes.

The young man died on the morning of March 5, 1890. Though he was only sixteen years old, newspapers throughout the United States announced his death. And not just because his father was the U.S. minister to Great Britain. It was because of the dead teenager's name: Abraham Lincoln.

No, this was not the legendary railsplitter who rose from the prairie to become president of the United States. This was his grandson—the grandson the president never knew, the grandson who never knew his famous ancestor. The boy who died on that bleak day in England was Abraham Lincoln II, born eight years after his grandfather's assassination. Known to friends and family as "Jack," he was "a grave boy," one of his teachers back in Chicago remembered. "He had much of the Lincoln blood in his veins." Like his grandfather, he was also athletic, "a large, strong fellow with good muscles," as someone who knew him recalled. The boy liked to ride horses and sail. He often took boat rides with his friend Abram

Jack posed for many photographs during his brief life. This 1889 profile was taken in Chicago, before his family moved to England.

Garfield, son of the twentieth president of the United States.

Jack especially loved to play baseball. It was said that one day, he or one of his pals hit a ball so far it broke a neighbor's window. The owner rushed angrily outside and demanded to know who had caused the damage. While the other boys scattered, Jack displayed the kind of honesty for which his grandfather was known, and quickly admitted guilt. Still furious, the man demanded to know his name. "Abraham Lincoln" came the answer. The owner grew pale, turned around, and rushed back inside his house without another word. One writer recalled that the man reacted as if he had seen a ghost.

For years, Jack also enjoyed reading. He could often be seen lying on the floor, books spread out before him, much as his celebrated grandfather had once sprawled with his books in front of his family's log-cabin fireplace. Jack especially enjoyed studying the Civil War and its greatest hero, his famous grandfather who was killed before he was born. He had even learned to imitate the president's familiar signature. In fact, Jack copied the handwriting so perfectly that years later, when people found a stack of long-forgotten books in the library of his father's summer home, all inscribed A. *Lincoln*, they believed they had discovered treasures actually signed by the dead president. Only later did they realize their mistake: the books had been published *after* Abraham Lincoln's assassination. This was Jack's mischievous work! All in all, Jack Lincoln was a clever, promising boy with a wonderful future ahead of him. Then, as had happened to other Lincoln boys before him, Abraham Lincoln II was struck down by tragedy—much too soon.

In truth, Abraham Lincoln II was not really the second but the *third* Abraham Lincoln.

Abraham Lincoln (1809–1865), sixteenth president of the United States, sat for this photograph in Washington in August 1863, just a few weeks after the Union triumph at the Battle of Gettysburg.

The first known Abraham Lincoln, a pioneer from Virginia, had been killed by an Indian war party near his cabin in Kentucky more than a century before, back in 1786.

His little son, Thomas, miraculously survived that attack and grew up to marry a girl named Nancy Hanks. They named their first son for the baby's murdered grandfather. As history so well remembers, the child was born in a tiny log cabin near the town of Hodgenville, Kentucky, on February 12, 1809. It was this second Abraham Lincoln who rose from prairie poverty to the White House and world fame.

The future President Lincoln, in turn, named his own firstborn son Robert. And years later when Robert fathered a son of his own, he named him Abraham Lincoln II, in honor of the late president. But like both of the Abraham Lincolns before him, this one also died too young. What was worse, with Jack's passing, the Lincoln name, too, came to a final end. All we have left of him are photographs: a strong-looking teenager riding on a horse or posing with a bicycle; or, in the end, a frail-looking child gazing up at the camera from the bed where he would later die. In these final poses, however, the boy looked astonishingly like his well-known grandfather!

But never again would there be a descendant of the great president bearing the name of Lincoln.

This is the story of the ill-fated Lincolns who came before Jack—not just the famous man who saved the Union and helped end slavery but his own four sons as well. This book will recall their own difficult lives, which were plagued by loneliness and despair or cut short by sickness and death.

This is the story of a family that might have enjoyed lifelong attention, wealth, and celebrity, but instead came to know sadness, illness, violence, and tragedy. This is the story of peaceful childhoods torn apart by a horrible war, of cousins and uncles who took sides against each other on bloody battlefields. And this is the story of great wealth made hollow by bitter feuding and public embarrassment. In the end, this is also a story about the high price of fame—what today we call "celebrity"—how quickly it can come and how rapidly it can disappear. For this is the story of the clan that might have become America's royal family but instead became America's cursed family—and then disappeared altogether.

This is the story of Lincoln's sons. It will tell not only how they died, but how they lived.

It begins with the most famous Lincoln of all: the future sixteenth president of the United States.

Jack is photographed at a studio with an outsize bicycle, a fake boulder, and a hunting horn as props. Note that the background is not real— but rather a curtain painted to look like the outdoors.

Abraham Lincoln stood six feet four inches.
He was the tallest president ever.

CHAPTER ONE
Mr. and Mrs. Lincoln: The Future Parents

Abraham Lincoln was a newly licensed lawyer and an up-and-coming politician when he decided to move from his home in the tiny village of New Salem, Illinois, and seek a new life in a bigger town. One spring morning soon thereafter, he arrived to live in nearby Springfield, the new capital of Illinois. The date was April 15, 1837. Lincoln was twenty-eight years old. Incredibly, he had exactly twenty-eight years left in his life—to the day! His great fame lay far in the future. But no one in this dusty little city would have predicted that this raw, strange-looking fellow would one day become the most famous man in America.

One visitor of the day called Springfield "a paradise in miniature." Lincoln had never lived in such a "busy wilderness," as he called it. But the tall, gangly state legislator did not much like his new hometown. He was impressed to see "a great deal of flourishing about in carriages." But even in a town crowded with people, he admitted: "I am quite as lonesome here as [I] ever was anywhere in my life." Always awkward with the opposite sex, Lincoln had difficulty meeting girls. "I have been spoken to by but one woman since I have been here," he reported to a lady friend he had once considered marrying, "and should not have been by her, if she could have avoided it." Lincoln was doing well enough as an attorney and legislator, but was finding social life a challenge.

Finally, probably sometime between 1837 and 1839, a beautiful young woman caught his eye. More important, he caught her eye as well. Mary Ann Todd had

Lincoln called his adopted hometown of Springfield, Illinois, a "busy wilderness" when he moved there at age twenty-eight in 1837. This view of its business district is one of the earliest-known photographs of the state's newly chosen capital city.

never met anyone quite so grotesque, yet quite so brilliant. And Lincoln had never met a girl so charming, yet so smart and opinionated.

As they soon discovered, they shared some important bonds. Like Lincoln, Mary hailed from the state of Kentucky (though Lincoln's clan had long ago moved into Indiana, then Illinois). On a more personal level, both of them had lost their mothers while children. The difference was that Abraham had come to love his kind stepmother, while, unfortunately, Mary never got along well with hers (perhaps because her stepmother started a large new family of her own with Mary's father). But there, the similarities ended.

Abraham's family had been dirt poor. Mary's father, Robert Smith Todd, was a wealthy and influential lawyer and businessman. The Lincolns always opposed slavery. But the Todds not only supported it but owned slaves themselves; enslaved people worked in the Todd household in the city of Lexington. Abraham admitted that he had been educated only "by littles." He had gone to school for barely a year during his entire childhood, though he made up for his lack of formal teaching by developing a huge appetite for reading. Mary had not only gone to boarding school; she had gone to college. She even learned to speak a little French.

In other ways, too, Abraham and Mary were total opposites. He was extremely tall and lean; she was short and a bit plump. He could go for hours without talking, or could read with total concentration no matter what was going on around him. She, on the other hand, loved to chatter away—and what was more, she expected to be answered! He was slow to anger; she was high-strung and excitable, easily offended, and nervous.

Mary Todd—the future wife of Abraham Lincoln—grew up in this fashionable home in Lexington, Kentucky, with many brothers and sisters. The Todd family owned slaves, who cooked and cleaned in this busy and crowded household.

He tended to be quite sad much of the time. By contrast, the dazzling Mary Todd was a hypnotic conversationalist—the life of every party she attended. Lincoln could certainly be a witty and fun-loving man, too—especially when spinning hilarious stories to other men, at which he would laugh as heartily as his listeners. Mary liked humor, too, but could often be sharp-tongued and sarcastic. During the times in which they lived, women were often criticized for having those qualities.

But the most dramatic difference of all between Abraham and Mary was obvious to anyone who saw them: he was not at all handsome, and she was quite pretty.

Though it doesn't show up in his photographs—many of which were retouched to make him look better (today we call the process airbrushing)—Lincoln was so ugly that he took to making fun of himself before others could do so. Often he told jokes in public about his appearance. For example, he loved telling the story of meeting an extremely homely old woman while riding his horse alone in the woods. Suddenly, the woman aimed a rifle at him and announced, "Prepare to die!" A frightened Lincoln begged to know, "why are you threatening me? I don't even know you." The reply came: "I once vowed that if I ever met a person uglier than I was, I would shoot him to death." To which, as Lincoln told his listeners, he replied: "Madam, if I am uglier than you are, then fire away!"

By contrast, Mary, who moved to Springfield to live with her sister, Elizabeth Todd Edwards, was always deeply concerned about her own appearance. She knew that her looks were her best quality. No one was surprised when Mary quickly became the belle of the city. She wore beautiful clothes and jewelry and took exquisite care of her hair, which she often decorated with fresh flowers. It is easy to understand why she became the center of attention at the best parties in town, fluttering her fan and winning the attention of many local gentlemen of marrying age.

Mary was so flirtatious, according to her brother-in-law, that she "could make a Bishop forget his vows." As one of her admirers declared, she was "the very creature of excitement," and she never enjoyed "herself more than when . . . surrounded by a company of merry friends." Mary was twenty-one in 1839—nine years younger than Abraham, but actually rather old for an unmarried girl of the time. Evidently she was willing to wait for the man of her dreams.

Legend holds that this odd couple met at one of those local parties where Mary always shone, and Lincoln usually hid from the ladies, content to swap stories with the men. But when he saw Mary, Lincoln summoned up his courage. He approached her cautiously and said, "Miss Todd, I want to dance with you in the worst way." And as Mary loved to recall of her clumsy admirer, "he certainly did!"

But even if they had little in common, it must be true that opposites attract. Something clearly sparked between them. Mary had moved to Springfield to meet the eligible bachelors there—especially the well-to-do lawyers and legislators who spent much of their time in the capital city. In fact, she could surely have had her pick of men there—even Stephen A. Douglas, the Democrat who would soon become Lincoln's main political rival and remain so for the next twenty years.

At the time, Douglas was much better known than Lincoln and far more successful. Quite short, but with a powerful physique and a strong voice, Douglas was already known to the state's voters by his nickname, "The Little

Stephen A. Douglas (1813–1861), Lincoln's lifelong political rival, was known as "The Little Giant." Douglas took a liking to Mary Todd before she became engaged to Lincoln, but Mary later scoffed that he was a "very little, *little* giant by the side of my tall Kentuckian."

Giant." But Mary found Abraham Lincoln far more appealing. She came to believe that the tall, poorly dressed lawyer had a far greater future ahead of him than even the well-known Douglas.

With "her head thrown back and her eyes shining with pride," she told a friend that Douglas seemed "a very little, *little* giant by the side of my tall Kentuckian." Intellectually, she added, Lincoln "towers above Douglas just as he does physically." But Mary's family did not share her enthusiasm. As one of the Todd relatives sniffed when it became clear that Abe Lincoln was the object of her affection, "in origin, in education, in breeding, in everything," Mary was by far the better catch. But Mary, who liked to tell friends and family that one day she would live in the White House as the wife of the president of the United States, believed Lincoln was more likely to fulfill her dream than anyone else she had ever known.

Perhaps the Lincoln-Todd romance really blossomed when they discovered that they shared a passion for two important things: Whig Party politics and serious poetry. Mary was such an ardent Whig supporter that even as a child she would stop playing and listen avidly to the great Henry Clay whenever he visited her father's home. Lincoln in turn believed deeply in the Whig Party platform, calling for the building of railroads and canals to link the nation's small towns closer together and provide jobs for all Americans. He must have been impressed by Mary's stories of meeting his hero, Senator Clay. Where poetry was concerned, Lincoln loved the rhymes of Robert Burns and the verse of William Shakespeare, and so did Mary. Later, the lovers would even try writing poetry of their own.

Soon the two were spending more and more time in each other's company. By late 1839, it was obvious to all their friends that they were courting. They had come to what was called "an understanding." "We were engaged & greatly attached to each other," remembered Mary. Abraham Lincoln and Mary Todd set January 1, 1841, as their wedding date.

What happened next no one really knows for sure—except that the marriage did not take place as scheduled. On what Lincoln later called the "Fatal First" of January, the groom either called off the ceremony or, worse, some whispered, cruelly left his bride at the altar. Had he fallen in love with someone else, as some have speculated? Did she get too angry at him for showing up late at a party—or did he become furious at her when he found her there flirting with other men? Was he worried he would be unable to support Mary in the lavish style to which she was accustomed? (As he put it: "I am so poor, and make so little headway in the world, that I drop back in a month of idleness, as much as I gain in a year's sowing." "It is bad to be poor," he later confessed.) Or, like many men, did Abraham Lincoln simply develop cold feet and a bad case of nerves? No one has ever learned the full truth. But Mary was certainly humiliated and hurt.

Feeling depressed and guilty, Abraham took to his bed. "I am now the most miserable man living," he confided. "If what I feel were equally distributed to the whole human family, there would not be one cheerful face on the earth." One friend insisted that "Lincoln went crazy as a loon" after breaking up with Mary. Another recalled that razors and other sharp objects were taken away from "his reach" out of fear he would try to harm himself—probably an exaggeration.

In any event, the couple stayed apart for months. Lincoln told his best friend, Joshua Speed, that he believed he could never again be happy because of "the never-absent idea, that there is *one*"—meaning Mary—"still unhappy whom I have contributed to make so. That still kills my soul." A fellow lawyer who saw the melancholy Lincoln after the breakup thought he seemed "emaciated in appearance" and "scarcely strong enough to speak above a whisper." An acquaintance jokingly predicted: "No more will the merry peal of laughter ascend *high in the air*"—a reference to the storyteller's great height—"to greet his listening and delighted ears."

To the folks in Springfield, Mary seemed equally unhappy. She moped and cried a good deal, bitterly complaining to a friend that her onetime fiancé now "deems me unworthy of notice." But she refused to seek new suitors. She preferred to hope for Lincoln to change his mind. Referring to a popular new version of *Richard II,* a famous Shakespeare play that the couple had probably once discussed, she expressed the hope that "Richard should be himself again." It is clear that, much as he had hurt her, Lincoln remained to Mary as majestic as that proud and self-confident English king.

Even if Abraham Lincoln believed he could not live with Mary Todd, he eventually came to the conclusion that he could not live without her either. Besides, he believed that he had promised her that they would marry and should live up to his offer. As he told Joshua Speed after Speed took a bride: "My old Father used to have a saying that 'If you make a bad bargain, hug it the tighter.'" Marriage might be a bad bargain, he joked, but it was also "the most *pleasant one . . .* which my fancy can, by any effort, picture."

When it became clear that Lincoln was softening, mutual friends brought the couple back together. Soon thereafter, they once again became engaged. After Josh Speed married his own fiancée first, Lincoln anxiously wrote to him to find out how their marriage was working out. Still unsure of himself, he desperately needed encouragement before taking the giant step himself. Lincoln asked Speed:

> *You have now been the husband of a lovely woman nearly eight months. That you are happier now than the day you married her, I well know . . . But I want to ask a close question—"Are you now in feeling as well as judgement glad that you are married as you are?" From any body but me, this would be an impudent question not to be tolerated; but I know you will pardon it in me. Please answer it quickly, as I feel impatient to know.*

Evidently, Speed's reply—now, unfortunately, lost—gave Lincoln all the confidence he needed. He finally made his move by sending Mary a set of recent election returns showing how the Whig Party was gaining strength in the community. Mary actually thought it a romantic gesture—perhaps only she would have felt so—and tied the bundle of papers with a pink ribbon.

Soon thereafter, Mary and her best friend, Julia Jayne, wrote a series of wicked comic poems for the local Whig newspaper. The poems poked fun at a conceited local Democrat named James Shields. The girls did not sign their names to the articles. When Shields took offense, Lincoln gallantly took the blame for the poems, and furious Shields challenged him to a duel. Lincoln went so far as to meet Shields on a nearby island in the Mississippi River, technically within the borders of Missouri, where dueling was legal. He was prepared to fight to defend his lady friend, until—thankfully—cooler heads won out and the fight was canceled.

His gallant gesture was more than enough for Mary. He was the husband for her. With none of the traditional notice to friends and relatives—neither set of parents was even invited—she and Lincoln scheduled their wedding for just after Election Day. This time there would be no long engagement. Mary would leave nothing to chance.

On a rainy November 4, 1842, nearly two years after they had first been scheduled to wed, Abraham and Mary asked a few friends to the parlor of the large Edwards home in Springfield for the long-delayed ceremony. There, thirty-three-year-old Abraham Lincoln married twenty-three-year-old Mary Ann Todd. She wore a borrowed white satin dress and a pearl necklace. A witness laughed that the groom looked "as pale and trembling as if being driven to slaughter." Engraved on the gold wedding band that the groom placed on Mary's finger were the words *Love is Eternal.*

"Nothing new here," Lincoln wrote a friend a few days later, "except my marrying, which to me is matter of profound wonder."

Within days, Mary was pregnant. To his friend Josh Speed, Lincoln soon hinted that there might soon be "a namesake at our house." The following July he sent Josh an update: "We are but two, as yet." But not for long.

After their marriage in 1842, Abraham and Mary Lincoln lived in
Springfield's Globe Tavern. Their first son, Robert, was born here
the following year. Mary later remembered, "a nice home-loving
husband and precious child are the happiest stages of life."

CHAPTER TWO
Two Become Four

The newlyweds moved into a room at the Globe Tavern, a noisy rooming house located in the heart of downtown Springfield. The plain-looking, two-story wooden building stood on Adams Street between Third and Fourth streets, not far from the site where the huge new statehouse was being built. How they chose it no one knows for sure, but one of Mary's sisters had lived there right after her marriage, too.

The inn offered eight rooms for rent upstairs, and the Lincolns moved into one of them, an eight-by-fourteen-foot bedroom with no bath and no parlor. Meals were included, along with laundry. As Lincoln put it: "We are not keeping house; but boarding at the Globe tavern, which is very well kept now by a widow lady of the name of [Mrs. Sarah] Beck. Our room . . . and boarding only costs four dollars a week."

But the couple paid another kind of price for this bargain. Downstairs, the Globe's busy first floor was reserved for group eating and drinking; there was little privacy. Also located on the street level were offices for various stagecoach lines. A deafening bell clanged every time a stage pulled up outside, no matter what the hour. Even worse, a blacksmith's shop operated next door, where hammering started early and ended late. It was hardly a quiet or romantic spot.

The new location was a vast upgrade for the husband—for he had long been sharing a crowded little loft above Josh Speed's store. But for his new wife—Lincoln lovingly called her "my Molly"—it was far less comfortable than the life she had left behind in her sister's glamorous mansion only a few blocks away, not to mention the Lexington, Kentucky, home where she had lived growing up.

Here at the modest and noise-filled Globe, the young couple began their married life. Their honeymoon, such as it was, was apparently successful! For here at the Globe, just nine months later, Mary gave birth to their first child, a son. They named him Robert Todd Lincoln, after Mary's beloved father, Robert Todd. Robert Lincoln came into the world on August 1, 1843.

Lincoln remembered waiting anxiously until he heard the newborn's "first squall." To a Springfield dentist, Lincoln joked: "I'm glad it is all over and that he is such a fine-looking little fellow. I was afraid he might have one of my long legs and one of Mary's short ones, and he'd have had a terrible time getting through the world."

According to Todd family tradition, Mary did not ask any of her three Springfield sisters to help her care for the newborn—who, friends noticed, had a slightly crossed left eye. Perhaps the Todd sisters had little time to spare. Older sister Elizabeth Edwards had just given birth to a baby of her own. Frances Todd Wallace had two infants in her care and a sick husband, too. And young sister Ann Todd was never very close to Mary to begin with; besides, the Lincolns thought her husband was "pretty much of a 'dunce.'"

Mary soldiered on alone. As a neighbor at the Globe remembered, "Mrs. Lincoln had no nurse for herself or for the baby. Whether this was due to poverty or to the great difficulty of securing domestic help, I do not know." Mary had no choice but to take care of little Bob, as his parents took to calling him, practically alone.

The neighbor who wrote that recollection was only six years old at the time. But she claimed that her mother taught Mary to bathe and dress the infant. Little Sophie Bledsoe recalled helping, too. "I was very fond of babies," she wrote years later, "and took on myself the post of amateur nurse. I remember well how I used to lug this rather large baby about to my great delight, often dragging him through a hole in the fence between the tavern grounds and an adjacent empty lot, and laying him down in high grass, where he contentedly lay awake or asleep, as the case may be." Mary never seemed very concerned. "I have often since that time wondered," Sophie admitted, "how Mrs. Lincoln could have trusted a particularly small six year old with this charge."

Perhaps Mary allowed such a young child to baby-sit because she was desperate for relief. Her husband was certainly not very helpful. Of course, fathers were not

The Lincolns moved here—the only home they ever owned—in 1844. It stood on the corner of Eighth and Jackson streets in Springfield. The photo on which this image was based was taken at least sixteen years later, by which time the family had added a second floor to the house and built a new kitchen in the back. Willie and Tad shared a bedroom upstairs; Robert had his own room, and Abraham and Mary had a two-bedroom suite.

expected to contribute to child care, according to the customs of the day. But Lincoln was not only unhelpful; he was absent. Quite busy again with his law practice, he worked constantly, often outside the town of Springfield. Mary was left to manage by herself, and her fellow boarders at the Globe remembered that Bob was not an easy baby. He cried often—and loudly.

Once the baby learned to walk, however, it became clear that the growing family could not continue to live at a tavern. So the following year, in 1844, the Lincolns paid twelve hundred dollars (plus a plot of land valued at another three hundred dollars) to buy a nearby one-and-a-half-story wooden home. It was owned by the minister who had pronounced them man and wife. The house stood (and still stands) on the corner of Eighth and Jackson streets. Here the Lincolns would live for the next seventeen years. Over time, the Lincolns greatly improved the place, adding a kitchen to the back and a full second floor with bedrooms for their children. They also built separate bedrooms for themselves—which in those days was more a sign of growing wealth than of declining love.

Things were in fact going very well for the young parents. Lincoln had left the state legislature after his marriage and was building his legal practice. In 1844, the longtime junior attorney opened his own law firm and took in a young man named William Herndon as *his* junior partner. Their partnership lasted until the day Lincoln left Springfield to become president of the United States. Yet Billy Herndon never joined the "family." Apparently, he once remarked to Mary at a party that she moved as sleekly as a serpent. Mary took it as a huge insult and never forgave him. Frowning on his weakness for liquor, she banished Herndon from her home. It proved to be one of her worst mistakes. Herndon became close to Lincoln and, decades later, would write a book about him. In it Herndon would describe Mary as a shrew who made her husband's life miserable. Herndon's vengeful words damaged Mary's reputation so severely that it never really recovered. Another fellow lawyer who knew Lincoln on the judicial circuit insisted that Lincoln "thoroughly loved his wife," even though he did not make a particularly "good husband."

Lincoln certainly was not fully satisfied merely practicing law. He continued to hunger for another chance in politics. In 1844, he tried hard to win the Whig Party nomination for the U.S. Congress, but lost to another candidate. Yet the party promised it would rotate the seat among other Whigs and that Lincoln's turn to run for Congress would come just two years later. And so it did.

A newspaper artist made this sketch of Lincoln's modest Springfield law office. It was plainly furnished but dirty. One visitor joked that a watermelon seed spat into a dusty corner in the winter took root and grew into a vine by spring.

The Lincolns named their second-born child, Eddy, after this man, Edward Dickinson Baker. Baker became a well-known western politician, U.S. senator from Oregon, and Civil War hero.

Recently discovered, some experts believe this is the only known photograph of Edward Baker Lincoln (1846–1850).

Lincoln was chosen to run for the seat in the U.S. House of Representatives in 1846 and began his campaign with high hopes for success. Before the race ended, yet another big event took place in the Lincoln house on Eighth and Jackson. On March 10, 1846, Abraham and Mary welcomed their second child into the world, another boy. His proud parents named the baby Edward Baker Lincoln—after a local politician they both admired, Edward Dickinson Baker. Lincoln had met Baker years earlier when both men served briefly in the Black Hawk War against regional Indian tribes. Unlike Lincoln, Baker had gone on to real military glory.

What was more, now he was serving as the congressman from Springfield, about to retire from the very seat for which Lincoln was running. It was little wonder that the couple chose him to be their new baby's namesake.

On August 3 of that same year—before little "Eddy," as they called him, sometimes spelling it "Eddie," was five months old—his father triumphed on Election Day. His victory was especially sweet. Lincoln became the only Whig elected to Congress from the entire state of Illinois in 1846. To celebrate, husband and wife put on their best clothes and went to the studio of a local photographer to have their pictures taken—their very first—separately. The daguerreotypes show a robust husband with sleek hair, enormous ears, and gigantic hands, and a pretty young wife wearing a striped dress and a cameo pin at her neck, her hair in curls.

Around the time he was elected to Congress, Abraham and Mary Lincoln posed for these daguerreotype portraits in Springfield. He was around thirty-seven, she twenty-eight. The couple never posed for a photograph together. Mary, much shorter, did not like the way they looked together.

In those days, newly elected congressmen were required to wait a full year and a half before starting their terms in Washington. So Lincoln went right back to his courtroom work. He began spending a good part of every month practicing law out of town, throughout the counties surrounding Springfield. This huge expanse of territory was known as the Eighth Judicial Circuit. Lawyers who lived in the center of the circuit could easily travel home for weekends. But Springfield lay at the southern tip of the vast circuit, and Lincoln usually found it less exhausting to stay on the road. Spending weekends on the circuit also meant that Lincoln had the time to make new friends

and win new supporters for future political campaigns. As a result, mother was now left to raise not one but two Lincoln boys without much help from their father.

In fact, father was away from home most of the time now, leaving Mary to keep house and care for the boys with no assistance except from an occasional maid. Lawyer Lincoln did get back home often enough to marvel at Eddy's rapid growth. In October, he wrote to Josh Speed to tell him: "We have another boy. . . . He is very much such a child as Bob was at his age—rather of a longer order." Apparently, Bob was short for his age.

Then Bob's father shared with his best friend the very first description he ever wrote about his older son. It was a remarkable letter, because just as he was writing it at his law office, Lincoln was interrupted by a family emergency. Bob had gone missing, and his always nervous mother was hysterical. Lincoln rushed home, discovered that Bob was back safely and the crisis over, and then calmly returned to work to finish his letter. Apparently, this was not unusual around Eighth and Jackson streets. Neighbors remembered how often they heard Mary Lincoln's voice shrieking: "Bobbie's lost! Bobbie's lost!"

Little else is known about the Lincoln family's early life, so this note offers a precious glimpse into the father's mixed feelings about his firstborn boy.

Sadly, between the lines, it is easy to see that Lincoln was just a bit disappointed in the three-year-old. Bob already seemed more his mother's son than his father's, more a Todd than a Lincoln. The boy was high-spirited and clever, all right, but for some reason, his father worried that he might become an early achiever who would soon flame out—harsh and stinging words indeed from any parent. This is what Lincoln bluntly wrote in October 1846:

> Bob is 'short and low,' and I expect, always will be. He talks very plainly—almost as plainly as any body. He is quite smart enough. I some times fear he is one of the little rare-ripe sort, that are smarter at about five than ever after. He has a great deal of that sort of mischief, that is the offspring of much animal spirits. Since I began this letter a messenger came to tell me, Bob was lost; but by the time I reached the house, his mother had found him, and had him whip[p]ed—and, by now, very likely he is run away again.

But it was the entire family that went away soon thereafter. The following fall—in October 1847—the Lincolns rented out their little house for a year, and then father, mother, and their two sons set out on a great adventure, leaving Springfield for the nation's capital. Their first trip to the city where they would later make history was about to begin. As Robert later modestly put it: "I followed the usual pursuits of infancy and childhood . . . until I was four years old, when I was taken by my parents to Washington, D.C."

But first they headed for three weeks' vacation at Mary's father's home in Lexington, Kentucky. It was a good opportunity for Bob and Eddy to enjoy the large Todd place, where they could play more freely and be spoiled by Grandfather Todd. They probably had to travel there by stagecoach, boat, and train. It was a grueling journey, and the strain of travel sometimes grew overwhelming.

A relative of Mary's stepmother, Betsy, happened to be riding on the very same train to Lexington and arrived at the Todd home just ahead of the Lincoln family. He had never met Mary, her husband, Abraham, or their boys. When someone there asked if he had enjoyed his ride, the young man exploded: "There were two lively youngsters on board who kept the whole train in a turmoil and their long-legged father, instead of spanking the brats, looked pleased as Punch and aided and abetted the older one in mischief."

At the very moment he was spinning this tale, he glanced outside the window, spied the Lincoln family approaching the house, and cried: "Good Lord, there they are now!"

Though Lincoln became a successful lawyer, pictures like this would never have been created had he not achieved national fame later. The lithographic print purports to show Lincoln arguing before the jury in the celebrated 1858 Duff Armstrong murder case—which he won. But Lincoln did not yet wear a beard in 1858—the picture actually shows him as he looked years later.

This daguerreotype by John Plumbe is the earliest-known photograph of the U.S. Capitol. It shows the building as it looked around the time Lincoln served as a congressman. The original dome was later replaced by a cast-iron one when Lincoln was president.

CHAPTER THREE
The Family Heads to Washington

The Lincoln family's long, exhausting journey to Washington resumed on November 25 and took around a week—a trip that today would require but a few hours by plane. The Lincolns probably set off by stagecoach from Kentucky to Virginia, where they picked up a railroad line toward Washington. In the 1840s, few railroads offered direct service; the family likely had to change trains more than once. The Lincoln brood finally arrived in the nation's capital on December 2 and booked a suite at Brown's Hotel while they looked for a more permanent home.

They found it right on Capitol Hill, in the shadow of the famous domed building where Congress met. The Lincoln family moved into Mrs. Ann G. Sprigg's large and comfortable boarding house, a convenient lodging that stood just across the plaza from the Capitol building. In fact, its spacious dining room—where all the boarders took meals together—overlooked the park, just a few yards from the Capitol's once famous iron fence. Today, the Library of Congress occupies the site where Congressman Lincoln, his wife, and their two little boys, Bob and Eddy, lived. Mrs. Sprigg's was a very popular residence for Whig congressmen from across the country. Edward Baker himself had lived there during his term and probably recommended it to Lincoln. The new representative much preferred it to the nearby boarding houses and hotels where other Illinois congressmen lived. He preferred dwelling with his fellow Whigs.

But not all of his fellow Whigs enjoyed living with the Lincolns. All ten residents were single or had left their wives and families back home. The Lincoln boys were the only children living there. It could not have been easy for the ever-proud Mary. Once again, she found herself living in a boarding house among strangers, just as she had the day she had married Lincoln. Robert later admitted he did not remember much about his first stay in Washington, but a doctor who lived at Mrs. Sprigg's remembered *him*. Congressman Lincoln's older boy, he recalled, was "a bright boy" who always "seemed to have his own way."

As the congressional session got underway across the plaza, Lincoln began boldly speaking out against the ongoing Mexican-American War. Not everyone agreed with him. Lincoln believed that the Democratic Party had misled the public about the reasons for going to war. He argued that Democrats planned the fight in order to capture new territory, which they planned to open to slavery. Even then, Lincoln opposed slavery and hoped it would someday cease to exist. He certainly did not approve of any schemes to spread it to new areas of the growing country.

In one speech, Lincoln even charged that the president of the United States, Democrat James Knox Polk, had faked a story about a Mexican attack on American soil as an excuse for invading Mexico. The representative from Springfield aroused much attention, not all of it positive. Lincoln's antiwar speeches were not well received back home. Many Springfield citizens, Democrats and Whigs alike, supported the president's policies or at least worried that Lincoln's speeches were disrespectful to soldiers fighting in the field.

Finding himself embroiled in the war when at work, Lincoln unfortunately found little peace when he was home. Mary was unhappy living at Mrs. Sprigg's. Though another boarder had described her similar lodgings as "a pleasant room on the second floor with a good bed, plenty of covering, a bureau table, chairs, closets—a good fireplace," Mary probably felt trapped there. She had two noisy toddlers to care for and few opportunities to attend parties like the other congressmen's wives.

She began suffering from daily headaches. Her children, particularly Eddy, ran so wild that they became the terrors of the boarding house. Mary was never easy to get along with in the best of circumstances. Now she began squabbling with some of the other boarders, who probably wanted more peace and quiet in their residence and blamed her for the children's constant noise. Since all the residents took meals together, it made living at Mrs. Sprigg's tense and miserable, especially when Lincoln was working long hours at the Capitol building.

Mary sought an escape from her routine. She took to shopping at Washington's fancy stores to relieve her boredom and unhappiness. She ran up large bills that the family could hardly afford. Often, when Mary ventured outside the boarding house, she left Bob and Eddy in the care of Mrs. Sprigg's servants—all of whom were slaves. At this very same time, her congressman husband was supporting a plan to abolish slavery in Washington. Lincoln was disappointed when it failed to pass the House. But if he ever felt unease about the slave-holding household in which his family now lived, he kept it to himself.

It seems likely that Eddy found it hardest of all to adjust to life in Washington. He was a sickly child, and the bad weather over the winter meant that Mary could seldom take him outside. Being trapped constantly indoors must have been especially difficult for the young child. And it must have been difficult for his mother—and the other residents—to live with an irritable, squirmy little boy. Some of the boarders thought it odd that Mary was still nursing her son, even though Eddy was nearly two years old. But Eddy seemed to need special attention. The boy missed his father badly whenever he went to work. But he could not pronounce the word *capitol*. Instead he said, "father has gone tapila," which his parents found cute.

By spring, Lincoln concluded that he could not serve Congress and his family at the same time. Congress won. In May 1848, he sent Mary and the boys away from "tapila." It is possible that Mary was ready for a change, anyway. Washington was not the city of her dreams, after all.

But where would she go now? The Lincolns had rented their home to someone else. So Mary packed up Bob and Eddy and headed back to Lexington to live with her father and the stepmother she disliked.

Hard as it was to have his family underfoot or to endure Mary's frequent complaints about being left alone when he went about his business, for Lincoln, it was harder to have them suddenly gone. He missed his wife and sons immediately—and immensely. "In this troublesome world," he admitted in a letter to his wife, "we are never quite satisfied. When you were here, I thought you hindered me some in attending to business, but now, having nothing but business—no variety—it has grown exceedingly tasteless to me. . . . I hate to stay in this old room by myself." Lincoln tried to be tactful when he reported to Mary about the other lodgers at Mrs. Sprigg's. "All the house—or rather, all with whom you were on decided good terms—send their love to you," he wrote, adding: "The others say nothing."

Lincoln particularly longed to see his boys and worried constantly that they would forget him. Though he hated shopping, and his wife had complained that he couldn't even tell one color from another until she taught him blue from pink, he now visited several Washington stores just to find the right plaid socks for "Eddy's dear little feet." He even proudly reported that he had picked out gold shirt studs for himself.

On one occasion, he had a frightening nightmare about Bob and wrote to Mary about it, worrying himself sick until she assured him that all was well in Kentucky. "I did not get rid of the impression of that foolish dream about dear Bobby till I got your letter," he wrote with relief, adding: "What did he and Eddy think of the little letters father sent them?" Above all, he begged his wife: "Don't let the blessed fellows forget father."

"Do not fear the children, have forgotten you," Mary reassured her gloomy husband from Lexington. "Even E[ddy's] eyes brighten at the mention of your name." Mary faithfully kept her husband aware of goings-on at her father's house, but not all the news she reported was pleasant. Eddy suffered "a little spell of sickness"—another sign of danger the parents perhaps did not quite understand. But the boy recovered. Mary wrote to Lincoln tenderly one night to assure him, "*our* babies are asleep."

On another occasion, as Mary unhappily reported, Bobby "triumphantly" brought home a kitten—"*your hobby*," she reminded Lincoln, who loved cats. Eddy was thrilled. His "*tenderness* broke forth," boasted his mother. He gave it water, "fed it with bread himself," and looked "delightful" as he held the kitten in his arms. But just as in a fairy tale, "in the midst of his happiness," Mary's stepmother walked in. She spied the mewing kitten and, being a cat-hater, ordered the servants to "throw it out." Even with "Ed screaming & protesting loudly," she recounted, "*she* never appeared to mind his screams, which were long & loud."

Most of the time, however, Mary seemed to get along fairly well with the stepmother she usually resented. They took carriage rides together, and "Ma" fed her the ice cream she loved. So Mary resisted the idea of traveling east again when her husband suggested that she return to Washington for a visit. "Come on just as soon as you can," he urged her on June 13, 1848. "I want to see you, and our dear— *dear* boys very much. Every body here wants to see our dear Bobby."

But Mary made no immediate effort to return her brood to hot, stuffy, unhealthy Washington. So, after complaining to Mary that he had received too many unexpected bills for purchases she had made before departing, Lincoln generously suggested she hire "a girl" to help her with the children. "Father expected to see you all sooner," he added with just a touch of resentment, "but let it pass; stay as long as you please, and come when you please. Kiss and love the dear rascals."

Finally, "Father" offered his family an irresistible excuse for a reunion: another adventure traveling around the country. For 1848 was a presidential campaign year, and Lincoln, the ever-loyal Whig, thought he must campaign actively for the party's new presidential nominee, General Zachary Taylor. At last, Mary and the boys eagerly journeyed back East, and then the entire family headed off in September for New England, where Lincoln planned to give speeches in support of Taylor.

The Lincolns headed north through New York City and then sped on to a number of villages in Massachusetts—including the town of Cambridge, where Bob would attend college years later. One newspaper reported enthusiastically that as a public speaker, this new man Lincoln was "hard to beat." Though Eddy suffered another bout of illness along the way, the family kept up their hectic pace. Their vacation was highlighted by an exciting visit to Niagara Falls, followed by a long boat cruise through the Great Lakes and on to Chicago before heading home. Even though travel was still extremely difficult at the time—requiring endless journeys on different railroads—the Lincolns seemed to enjoy their tiring trip. Not until October 10 were they reported back at last in Springfield. Even the city's Democratic Party newspaper, which seldom had anything good to say about Lincoln, admitted that the congressman looked "remarkably well."

Lincoln did not run that year for reelection to a second term in Congress. Some writers have argued that he failed to get another chance because he had become unpopular after speaking out against the Mexican-American War. But the truth is, Lincoln had agreed two years earlier to let someone else have a chance at the Whig nomination in 1848. Such was the same system of "rotation" under which he had earned the opportunity to run two years before. In the end, to no one's surprise, another Whig earned the nomination for U.S. representative. But he lost his election. Lincoln's congressional seat went to the Democrats, and some Whigs at home put the blame on Lincoln for driving pro-war voters away from the party.

General Zachary Taylor, a Mexican War hero, was the Whig Party candidate for president in 1848. Congressman Lincoln supported him enthusiastically, making speeches on his behalf in the East. But when Taylor won the White House, the new president did not appoint Lincoln to the kind of job the Illinoisan thought he deserved.

If Lincoln was happy to be home for a while, away from politics, his good humor faded soon thereafter. Though Zachary Taylor won the White House, the new president failed to reward Lincoln with a political job he believed he deserved—the post of commissioner of the General Land Grant office. The job would have required the family to move to Washington again, this time permanently. But it was an important post, and surely the Lincolns would become important residents of the capital. It was not to be.

Someone else got the job. To console the disappointed Lincoln, President Taylor offered him a different one—but in a distant, remote place. Lincoln could have the post of governor of the new territory of Oregon. The job paid a good salary for the times: three thousand dollars a year! Of course, Oregon was the most northwestern slice of land in the entire country. But anyone who took the job of governor would instantly become the most important citizen of the territory, perhaps, in time, its first United States senator. And that was an honor Lincoln always thirsted for the most. Bob and Eddy would have probably loved to move to the exciting West. If Lincoln ever seriously considered the job, however, Mary soon put her foot down: she absolutely refused to leave Springfield behind and uproot her family to move so far away. She would not go to Oregon, and in the end, neither did her husband.

Considering himself a political failure, Lincoln returned to Washington for his final lonely months as a congressman. The excitement was gone. He was now a "lame duck," a man still holding office but scheduled to depart. With scarce prospects for the future, he realized he would soon have to retire from politics altogether—at least for the time being. Back home in Springfield once again, this time for good, he believed, he resumed his legal practice. Mary moved the family back into their house, and though her lawyer husband again began traveling throughout the enormous Eighth Judicial Circuit—fourteen counties in all—for long periods of time, she had become used to his absences. "Mr. L. is not at home," she told one of her half sisters in a typical letter. "This makes the fourth week. . . . " Yet in a way, the Lincolns seemed happier than they had ever been before. The boys were growing fast and no doubt glad to be home.

But then tragedy struck. And things were never quite the same for the Lincoln family again.

Mary Lincoln did not like this photograph of her husband. The future president thought she objected to the "disordered condition" of his hair. According to legend, Lincoln arrived at Alexander Hesler's Chicago gallery looking neat and combed. But the photographer ran his fingers through his subject's hair to make him look more interesting.

CHAPTER FOUR
"We Miss Him Very Much"

The family actually suffered more than one painful tragedy as the 1840s ended and the 1850s began. First, Mary's beloved father, Robert Todd, died of cholera in July 1849. His two sets of children—sixteen in all from two different wives—commenced to fight bitterly over his will. The Lincolns again traveled, this time to Lexington, to protect their rights in the ugly legal battle over the Todd money. Once more, Eddy was uprooted and taken on yet another long and exhausting journey. In his brief time on earth, the little boy traveled thousands of miles. It did him little good. Eddy was home for only about half of his life.

The Lincolns retuned to Springfield, richer than ever before, with an inheritance in hand from Mary's father. But their joy did not last long. Eddy was growing sicker by the day. Doctors at the time did not understand childhood diseases, much less know how to treat them successfully. We are still not certain exactly what illness plagued little Eddy. But according to records of the day, he probably had consumption, what today we call tuberculosis—and can easily cure using modern methods. Without proper treatment (and none was available in the Lincoln era), the disease fills the lungs with fluid until the patient all but drowns in his own body.

A worried Abraham Lincoln, for once, spent less time at work and more time at home, fretting over his suffering child. For her part, Mary tried desperately to nurse her little boy back to health. She sat with him, read to him, rubbed his chest with balsam, and tried to get him to eat. But he only grew weaker. Eddy had survived health crises before. But this time, his body was too weak and he did not rally. Before daybreak on the cold, rainy morning of February 1, 1850, the little boy died in the same house on Eighth and Jackson streets where he first saw life. He had been sick for a full month and a half. Edward Baker Lincoln was just a few weeks shy of four years old, a birthday he would never get to celebrate.

Abraham and Mary were devastated. Always in control of his emotions, Lincoln now cried openly. On one occasion he was seen reading a little card he had found on a table at home: it was a prescription for some new medication to help the ailing boy—too late to be filled. "He looked at it—then threw it from him and bursting into tears left the room." Mary in turn grieved so hard she could not be consoled. She cried constantly and refused food, until her husband begged her: "Eat, Mary, for we must live." Three weeks after Eddy's funeral, which took place inside their own parlor, Lincoln wrote to his stepbrother to break the horrible news with simple and heartfelt words: "I suppose you had not learned that we lost our little boy. He was sick fifty-two days & died the morning of the first day of this month. . . . We miss him very much."

Somehow, the sad parents were able to express their grief in much the same way they had expressed their love years earlier: through poetry. On February 7, less than a week after the boy's death, the local newspaper printed a sad poem called "Little Eddie." No author was identified. But because the poem is so similar in rhythm to other rhymes by Lincoln, and because it features phrases that Mary often used to describe her children (like "angel child"), only one explanation is possible: mother and father composed it together. Perhaps it helped them through their grief.

The poem (see page 45) tells us much about how parents of those times—particularly the Lincolns—reacted to the death of their youngsters. It was hardly uncommon in the mid-nineteenth century for parents to lose children. Modern medicine had not been invented yet, and simple colds often led to pneumonia and death. Water was untreated and often unsafe, and many children developed fatal diseases from drinking it. Their deaths were always sad, but seldom surprising. Countless families suffered the loss of children in the Lincoln era.

Ministers of the mid-nineteenth century tried to ease the grief of such mothers and fathers by assuring them that their children would be happier and safer after death than they had been in life—that they were too good for the world and were better off in God's hands in a perfect heaven. Surely Dr. James Smith, the town's new Presbyterian minister who performed Eddy's funeral service, offered just such a message to the Lincolns. One certainly hears such religious beliefs echoed in the poem "Little Eddie."

But the poem also offers us some clues about the Lincoln boy's suffering and

LITTLE EDDIE

Those midnight stars are sadly dimmed,
That late so brilliantly shone,
And the crimson tinge from cheek and lip,
With the heart's warm life has flown—
The angel of Death was hovering nigh,
And the lovely boy was called to die.

The silken waves of his glossy hair
Lie still over his marble brow,
And the pallid lip and pearly cheek
The presence of Death avow.
Pure little bud in kindness given,
In mercy taken to bloom in heaven.

Happier far is the angel child
With the harp and the crown of gold,
Who warbles now at the Saviour's feet
The glories to us untold.
Eddie, meet blossom of heavenly love,
Dwells in the spirit-world above.

Angel boy—fare thee well, farewell,
Sweet Eddie, We bid thee adieu!
Affection's wail cannot reach thee now
Deep though it be, and true.
Bright is the home to him now given
For of such is the Kingdom of Heaven.

Halliday & Kessberger

SPRINGFIELD, ILL.

The Lincolns worshipped at this Presbyterian church in Springfield. Mary joined the congregation, but Abraham never became a member.

death. It refers, for example, to a "crimson tinge from cheek and lip." Eddy's face must have turned quite red with high fever in his final days. Then the verse describes the boy's "marble brow." This probably means that the Lincolns put the child in a small coffin and laid it out in their parlor—very common in that period—leaving the lid open so visitors could view the tiny body before his burial. The dead boy must have looked like a small marble statue to his sad parents.

How Mary recovered from such a terrible ordeal no one is sure. In a way, she never did. Friends remembered her grief often giving way to hysteria. Mary did become a member of Rev. Smith's Presbyterian church, located just a few blocks from the Lincoln home. Obviously, the preacher had offered her some comfort. But even though her husband occasionally joined her in her pew for Sunday services, Lincoln never took out a membership for himself. In fact, he never belonged to any church from that time until the end of his own life.

Worship and faith in God could help only so much. Mary never forgot her precious second son or got over his loss. For years, it was thought that she never even had a photograph of her dead child to remember him by. Recently, a photo came to light that some historians believe shows Eddy as he looked shortly before his death. If so, having such a keepsake must have been a comfort to his unhappy parents.

But no image could replace the living child. As late as the summer of 1853, Mary could still vividly recall "our second boy, a promising bright creature of four years we were called upon to part with several years ago." As she added: "I grieve to say that even at this day I do not feel sufficiently submissive to our loss."

Even many years later, when Mary was living in the White House, a young girl remembered the First Lady as still very eager to tell her, a near stranger, all about Eddy's brief life. And then, as the girl fondly recalled "we wept together as she told me about his death."

But within weeks of Eddy's passing in 1850, there was more talk of life than of death inside the Lincoln home—more talk of a brighter future, perhaps, than the tragic past. Mary was again pregnant. Soon the Lincolns would welcome another boy to replace little Eddy . . . if he could.

This is believed to be the only photograph of Abraham Lincoln's father, Thomas. The two were not close, and Abraham did not visit him at his deathbed or place a headstone on his grave.

CHAPTER FIVE
Enter Willie and Tad

The third Lincoln boy came into the world as his parents' early Christmas present. He was born four days before the holiday, on December 21, 1850. The happy mother well remembered how caring and helpful her sister Frances's husband, a doctor, had been when Eddy had been born—and when he had died. In honor of their brother-in-law Dr. William Wallace, Abraham and Mary named their new baby William Wallace Lincoln. But they would always call him "Willie."

The next summer, Mary proudly took Bob and his new young brother, Willie, off to her stepmother's for a vacation at the Todd home in Kentucky. There, Bob happily "scampered about on ponies, slid down the ice-house roof and romped with the dogs." For the most part, Little Willie was left in the care of "Aunt Sally," the house slave who had once been Mary's own "nanny." It was not the first time Mary had used slaves to help care for the sons of the man who would one day help end slavery. Once again, Mary let herself be pampered by slave labor, feeling no guilt. Meanwhile, Bob found new playmates and new places to explore.

Returning home to Springfield, Bob began attending a local school known as Mr. Estabrook's Academy, as well as Sunday school at the First Presbyterian Church. He was not exactly studious, though he did manage to retain some things from the beloved books his mother tried to share with him. Together with his mother, he read the famous English adventure novels by Sir Walter Scott. For a time, Mary worried that Robert did not share her affection for these romantic stories of knights and their ladies. But one day, she learned otherwise after she heard a noisy brawl coming from outside their home.

Leaning out of their window, she saw young Bob brandishing a wooden fence rail—his version of a lance—and shouting a famous line from Scott's romance *The Lady of the Lake* at a frightened playmate: "'This rock shall fly from its firm base as soon as I.'" Laughing, Mary recited a line of her own, an effort to break up the fight: "'. . . brave knights. Pray be more merciful than you are brawny.'" Discipline was the last thing on Mary's mind that merry day. The Lincolns were becoming a family again.

The family was soon to grow by one more. Less than three years after Willie's arrival, the Lincoln home again echoed with the cries of a newborn baby. After three boys, Mary had desperately yearned for a girl at last, but on April 4, 1853, she instead bore her fourth son. It was a difficult labor and an extremely painful childbirth. The baby's head was so big that instruments may have been used to help extract him. In those days, such tools were not even sterilized. It is highly possible that the birth caused Mary internal injuries. She would suffer from so-called women's troubles for the rest of her life. And worse than that, she was told she could never have another baby. Mary Lincoln's child-bearing years were over. She was only thirty-four years old.

The parents called their new child Thomas Lincoln, after the future president's father. But he was an odd-looking baby—with a gigantic head atop a tiny, squirming body. The father thought that the new arrival looked like a baby frog— a tadpole. Then and there, as Mary remembered, the baby "was *nicknamed*, Taddie, by his loving Father." From that moment on, he was "Tad" or "Taddie" to his parents and eventually to the rest of the country, too.

Perhaps they settled on a nickname, in part, because *Thomas* was such a peculiar choice for a name in the first place. Abraham Lincoln had not been at all close to his late father. Just a few years before, back in January 1851, when the old man lay dying, Lincoln refused his plea to come home to bid him farewell. As he explained to his stepbrother, Mary had just given birth to Willie and was herself "sick abed," suffering from what he described as "baby-sickness."

But there was more to his refusal than Mary's illness. As Lincoln went on to admit, he believed a reunion with his father would be "more painful than pleasant." The elder Thomas Lincoln died on January 17, 1851, without ever again seeing his only living child. Lincoln did not even attend the funeral or order a gravestone for his father's burial plot. Baby Thomas would never meet the grandfather for whom he was named. Perhaps the Lincolns, Abraham in particular, gave him the name out of guilt.

Sarah Bush Johnston Lincoln, Thomas's second wife and beloved stepmother of the future president.
She outlived her famous stepson by four years.

The "traditional" Abraham Lincoln log cabin birthplace now sits in a large marble temple in Hodgenville, Kentucky. But it is probably not authentic. When the History Channel recently conducted tests on the logs, it found the wood to be only about one hundred years old.

None of the Lincoln boys—or Mary herself—ever laid eyes on Abraham Lincoln's father or the stepmother he adored. Nor did they ever glimpse his old prairie home. Many historians believe that Mary did not want her sons to be exposed to the squalid log cabin where her husband had once lived. To her (and later, to Bob, who took after his mother in so many ways), Abraham's origins were to be forgotten, not celebrated. The same went for the simple relatives Lincoln left behind.

It was not until two years after the president's death that Mary would reach out for the very first time to contact her late husband's beloved old stepmother, Sarah Bush Johnston Lincoln. Mary finally felt the need to tell the elderly woman: "Perhaps you know that our youngest boy, is named for your husband, Thomas Lincoln, this child, the idol of his father." This was an astonishing admission. Distant from her own stepmother, Mary made no effort to know her husband's stepmother either.

After Tad's birth, Mary was soon happily describing herself as "the mother of three noisy boys," even though they were hard to handle, particularly "our *dear little Taddie*."

Still, just six days after Tad's birth, Lincoln returned to the legal circuit. His wife was still suffering the aftereffects of Tad's painful delivery, but Lincoln would remain away from home for some two months. Once again, Mary was left to fend for herself, sometimes with the help of live-in maids, who would often flee under Mary's harsh criticism. Mary was never happy living alone—particularly during thunderstorms, which she feared and hated—but she had little choice. Lincoln needed to earn a living, and his law career required him to travel.

The increasingly nervous mother did try to remain especially close to her oldest boy. Bob had troubles, too, emotional as well as physical. He had suffered a terrible loss of his own when Eddy died; a brother and a playmate had vanished forever. Now, when he was seven years old, a new baby had arrived, taking much of his mother's attention. Soon thereafter came Tad. The youngest boys were as close in age as Bob and Eddy had been and would soon become each other's best friend. In a way, Bob was left out.

The boy attended local schools in Springfield, but the other students there teased him endlessly and called him "cockeye," until his mother saw to it that he had a painful operation to correct his vision. Bob in turn became a terrible tease himself, who "delighted in tormenting his mother," as a neighbor testified. Left alone to manage her active boys, Mary became the family disciplinarian.

Lincoln was a self-made man. In his youth, and before he entered politics, young Abe was a flatboat pilot.

Both parents desired that Bob have a good education. Mary wanted him to have the same advantages she had, and Abraham was just as determined his son enjoy all the opportunities he had lacked. Mary even enrolled him in a dancing class. As the oldest, Bob was also given responsibilities at home. Often the boy was left in charge of his two younger brothers when his parents went out at night on social calls. But Bob was powerless to keep Willie and Tad out of mischief, and they often escaped the house and wandered the streets in search of their parents. The two sleepy youngsters showed up uninvited to one late-night party—Tad with his trousers on backward.

If he was home in Springfield, Lincoln tried to be there for all the boys—unless Mary lost her temper. Whenever "Mrs L got the devil in her," a friend reported, "Lincoln . . . would pick up one of his Children & walked off—would laugh at her—pay no Earthly attention."

The truth was, Mary was not only prone to anger, but helpless in a crisis. Once, when Bob swallowed some poisonous lime stored in the family outhouse, all she could do was scream, "Bobbie will die!" One of her neighbors heard her wailing, rushed over, and washed out Bob's mouth. Mary could easily have done so herself, but she panicked. As usual, Lincoln was traveling at the time.

With his father so often absent, it is no real surprise that Bob began behaving more like his mother. He developed a temper of his own. One evening, Mary sent the boy to fetch his father for dinner. Lincoln was busy in his office—busy, that is, playing a game of chess with a judge named Samuel Treat. Bob told his father to come home and then retreated back to the house. But minute after minute passed, and still Lincoln failed to show up. Growing angrier, Mary demanded that Bobby go back and bring his father home without fail.

The boy returned to the offices of Lincoln & Herndon to discover the chess game still in progress. Bob repeated his mother's orders that Lincoln come home to dinner. But again, his father ignored him, deeply focused on his match. So Bob simply strolled up to the chessboard and with all his might kicked it into the air, scattering the chess pieces. All Lincoln did was rise from his seat and calmly declare: "Well, Judge, I reckon we'll have to finish this game some other time." (Some writers have told this same story with Tad kicking the chessboard.)

Both parents encouraged all their children to be imaginative and run free, but Abraham worried less about them than Mary did—sometimes with disastrous results. Once, Lincoln became so preoccupied he actually became guilty of what today we would call child neglect! On the day in question, he was cheerfully pulling one of his younger children down the street in a wagon, "pretending to be the pony." But according to the famous story, he soon forgot all about the baby, who fell out of the wagon and lay crying on the ground as Lincoln walked on, lost in his own thoughts. The absentminded father "did not realize that he was pulling an empty wagon" and "had dumped the little driver, who was left kicking and squalling in the gutter."

Luckily—at least for the baby, not his father—Mary miraculously appeared on the street, saw what had happened, screamed in horror, and ran to the child's aid. After rescuing him, she turned her full fury on Lincoln and gave her husband a sound tongue-lashing in full view of passersby. Embarrassed, Lincoln fled the scene, "his long legs taking him out of sight."

It comes as no surprise that, to their neighbors and relatives, Mr. and Mrs. Lincoln's relationship seemed to have its full share of ups and downs. Sometimes the two were seen holding hands and laughing together. But angry words were often heard from their home, too—always coming from wife, not husband—and on several occasions, people observed Mary chasing Lincoln down the street (once waving a broom at him) or shouting at him to return inside.

But much as they remained opposites in personality, these two unusual people shared a deep and unbreakable love for their boys. They simply showed their devotion in different ways. Mary clung to the children, fussed over them, worried about them, lost her temper at them, and then made up with them and hugged them ever closer. By contrast, Lincoln was patient and serene—but, of course, he was at home so seldom that he could always be the "good" parent.

When the family dog took a bite out of little Bob, Mary shrieked with worry that the boy might get rabies but had no idea of what to do. Lincoln calmly took the pet away with Bob in tow and left the pet with another family—in Indiana! While there, he made sure that doctors there examined the boy and pronounced him to be in good health.

Of course, Lincoln always preferred cats to dogs anyway. But he could not have been pleased when Bob was once discovered harnessing dogs to wagons.

Mary found the boys hard to control when Lincoln was on the road. Their servant Margaret Ryan insisted, "Mrs. L would whip Bob a good deal." Margaret even claimed that the temperamental Mary occasionally struck her servant girls, too.

One thing mother and father agreed on—at least in theory—was how to raise their boys. They were both what today we call "permissive" parents. That is, they believed that their children should run free, even wild, even if their behavior disturbed or horrified everyone else around them. "Spare the rod and spoil the child," Lincoln once confidently declared. "Spare the rod for you may warp the child's personality." Lincoln's father had beaten him as a young man, and he never got over the experience. He was not about to inflict any physical punishment on his own sons, ever. Mary was less successful than Abraham in controlling her temper, and while she did not always "spare the rod," she was never spare with her love and affection. A neighbor remembered that when the children and their friends became "boisterous," Mary did not usually scold them. Instead she gave them cookies.

Mary herself was the first to recognize what a special parent her husband became. She called him "the most loving husband and father in the world," adding: "He gave us all unbounded liberty. . . . He was very—exceedingly indulgent to his children." Mary recalled Lincoln once remarking: "'It is my pleasure that my children are free, happy, and unrestrained by paternal tyranny. Love is the chain whereby to lock a child to its parent.'" With affection and patience, Lincoln locked his children to his side.

But not everyone appreciated the way the Lincolns reared the younger boys. Chaos and destruction was often the result of Lincoln's reluctance to impose discipline. On many Saturdays, for example, when Willie and Tad acted up and their mother could no longer control them, the exhausted Mary often asked her husband to take them with him to his law office. She desperately needed such breaks.

But once inside the firm of Lincoln & Herndon, Willie and Tad ran amok. Law partner William Herndon was horrified when the "little devils," as he called them, invaded the workplace he labored hard to keep well organized. "They soon gutted the room," he remembered bitterly, "gutted the shelves of books, rifled the drawers, and riddled boxes, battered the points of my gold pens against the stairs, turned over the inkstands on the papers, scattered letters over the office, and danced over them."

As Herndon seethed, "had they shat in Lincoln's hat and rubbed it on his boots, he would have laughed and thought it smart."

Herndon admitted: "I have felt many and many a time that I wanted to wring their little necks . . . wring the necks of these brats and pitch them out of the windows. . . . [Y]et out of respect for Lincoln I kept my mouth shut." Lincoln was simply "blinded to his children's faults," his partner insisted (no doubt jealous of all the attention and all the praise he lavished on the obnoxious boys). "He worshipped his children and what they worshipped; he loved what they loved and hated what they hated." To Herndon, this was a fault. To modern families, it would probably be regarded as a virtue.

One of Lincoln's oldest friends glimpsed the more tender side of Lincoln's parenting style. He "would take his Children and would walk out on the Rail way out in the Country—would talk to them—Explain things Carefully—particularly. He was Kind—tender and affectionate to his children—very—very."

Once, Lincoln proudly took Bob to a secluded forest where, as a young man, he had helped to survey some land. Somehow recognizing the terrain and pointing to a thicket of trees, the father escorted his boy into the woods, describing one specific tree that Lincoln had long ago marked as a guidepost. Sure enough, Bob found it exactly where his father said it would be. "[H]e never made a mistake," Lincoln's oldest boy remembered. Lincoln always took the time to instruct Bob— and to calmly correct him if he was mistaken about something, even when Mary angrily defended the boy.

Lincoln was "the very best and Kindest and father I ever saw," agreed Mary's sister Frances. "He was a domestic man . . . was always at home if in town." The trouble was, he was in town so seldom.

The father enjoyed pampering, even spoiling, his boys. One day Frances scolded him for carrying Tad around Springfield. "Why, Mr. Lincoln," she said, "put down that great big boy. He's big enough to walk." To which Lincoln replied: "Oh, don't you think his little feet get too tired?" On another occasion, Tad scampered into his father's office to complain that his big brother Bob had forced him to trade his new knife for a pocketful of candy. When Bob appeared, Lincoln shamed him into returning the knife, explaining, "it's a big thing for him . . . the first knife Tad ever had." Bob sheepishly handed it over, and then the lawyer father instructed Tad to return the candy "to make things square between you."

"I can't," Tad answered, "'cause I ate up all the candy Bob give me, and I ain't got no money to buy it." With a laugh, Lincoln gave up trying to teach them a lesson and took both boys to the store to purchase more sweets.

Both mother and father simply loved showing off their children—dressing them up and often asking them to recite or perform before audiences that seldom shared the parents' enthusiasm. Lincoln's law partner, Herndon, for one, complained that Mary would "trot out Bob—Willie and Tad, and get them to monkey around—talk—dance—speak—quote poetry . . . much to the annoyance" of her bored guests.

———————◆▸✕◂◆———————

Life for the Lincoln family changed dramatically in 1854—but this time the cause was political, not personal. That year—when Bob was eleven, Willie four, and Tad one—Congress passed a new law called the Kansas-Nebraska Act. Its author was none other than Senator Stephen A. Douglas, the man once rumored to have been in love with young Mary Todd.

Douglas's law gave white residents in the country's new western territories the right to hold special elections to vote on whether to allow slavery. The old Missouri Compromise laws, which had long kept slavery limited to the South, were overturned. The senator called the new scheme "popular sovereignty."

Popular sovereignty outraged Lincoln. He believed it was a scheme meant to clear the path to spread slavery nationwide, North as well as South. For the first time since his retirement from Congress, he decided to return to politics. He now had a cause that *aroused* him to action, as no other issue had in his lifetime: preventing the spread of slavery, and guaranteeing freedom and opportunity for new generations of Americans.

Lincoln's political comeback would give much to the nation but take much away from his family. As he began giving speeches once again throughout Illinois, the ever-busier Lincoln found he had less time than ever to spend with his wife and children. This caused pain for the father, created new burdens for the mother, and left the boys more uncontrollable than ever.

Politics remained a major challenge as well. Lincoln worked hard to win a seat in the United States Senate in 1855 but failed when the state legislature, which then elected senators, chose someone else. The struggle against slavery would not be easy.

By then, the old Whig Party was dying, so Lincoln joined the new Republican Party. In 1858, he became its candidate for another U.S. Senate seat—this time requiring him to run against his old foe, Stephen A. Douglas. That summer and fall, Lincoln and Douglas met in a series of seven political debates. These appearances won widespread attention not only in Illinois but throughout the nation. The Lincoln-Douglas debates, as one reporter wrote, set the prairies "on fire." Fifteen-year-old Bob got to attend the three-hour-long final debate at the river town of Alton, Illinois. The excited teenager was dressed in a corporal's uniform, as a member of a youth group called the Springfield Cadets.

In one sense, the long political campaign ended in failure. Lincoln lost yet again, and Douglas was reelected to another term in the Senate. Asked how he felt about the experience, Lincoln said he was too sad to laugh, but too big to cry. But as the defeated candidate and his family were soon to learn, he had won something even greater than a Senate seat: national fame. Newspapers around the country had covered the Senate campaign and reprinted Lincoln's debates with Douglas. Denied victory, Lincoln earned attention and praise.

The Lincoln boys' father was now a national celebrity.

In 1858, Abraham Lincoln and Stephen A. Douglas debated seven different times during their hotly contested race to represent Illinois in the U.S. Senate. Their joint outdoor appearances were attended by tens of thousands of people and remain the most famous political debates in American history.

This ambrotype (a photo on glass) is one of the earliest-known photographs of Robert Lincoln, then age fifteen. Noting his resemblance to his mother, a neighbor remarked that Bob was "a Todd, in appearance and disposition."

These early ambrotypes of nine-year-old Willie (left, 1850–1862) and six-year-old Thomas "Tad" Lincoln (1853–1871) were taken around 1859 and lovingly preserved in this beautiful double frame. Mary took the pictures with her to Washington in 1861.

CHAPTER SIX
The House Dividing

When Lincoln won the nomination to run for the Senate in June 1858, he gave a famous speech in Springfield in which he repeated this phrase from the Bible: "A house divided against itself cannot stand."

What Lincoln meant was that America could no longer exist "half *slave* and half *free*." He feared that the national house was splitting in two over the issue of slavery. "It will become *all* one thing," he predicted, "or *all* the other."

The Lincolns' own house was not exactly falling apart. But things had never seemed so difficult and uncertain. Father and mother had good reason that year to wonder what would happen not only to the United States but also to their own little family. Where would the voters—and history—take them next? And could a household of growing boys who needed their father survive Abraham Lincoln's ever more frequent absences from home?

What did the three Lincoln boys look like at the time? "While I was a boy at Springfield," Bob later recalled, a "new process came in, called the ambrotype." These were photographs made on glass plates, mounted in shiny brass frames, and encased in leather or thermoplastic cases that opened like little books. Only one copy could be produced of each picture, and families treasured the precious images and kept them on display in their homes. The Lincolns embraced the new technology. Robert sat for his first photograph around 1858. It shows a dignified-looking boy with thick, pomaded (gelled) hair, a fine suit of clothes, and only one defect to mar his perfect appearance: a big, sloppily knotted bow tie. A friend of the family described Robert at the time as "like his mother, a Todd, in appearance and disposition."

The Lincolns made sure their younger boys were photographed, too. Their earliest ambrotypes show Willie looking serious and Tad impish, as if he were about to jump out of his chair and trash the photographer's studio. Both pose with big hats, fancy jackets, and shirts with white collars. Tad's collar is made of lace—perhaps stitched by his mother, who sewed beautifully. Looking at him, one would think he was as well behaved as a choir boy.

Unlike most couples at the time, Abraham and Mary never posed for a photo together. Some said it was because Mary was so much smaller than her husband that she feared such pictures would make her appear ridiculous. Yet many tall husbands of the day posed with shorter wives with no such embarrassment—because the man usually sat in a chair while the woman stood next to him. Mary probably refused to have her picture taken for another reason: she simply did not like the way photographs made her look. Her hands, she later explained, always came out looking too large. Besides, Lincoln had most of his own photos taken in cities other than Springfield. The reason for that was simple. More and more often, he was away from home, alone.

As 1858 turned into 1859, Lincoln not only continued to practice law, more successfully than ever. But he also toured the state and the region in search of support for the Republican Party and the idea of halting slavery's spread. The cause now came first; his family, second. He grew famous for the unique style of his antislavery speeches, filled with humor and logic. No one in the country shot down Stephen Douglas's ideas more brilliantly than Abraham Lincoln. Huge and enthusiastic crowds cheered him wherever he went. But often his own wife did not know precisely where he was.

In February 1859, for example, Mary had no choice but to write to one of Lincoln's close friends in an effort to find her husband.

> *If you are going up to Chicago to day, & should meet*
> *Mr. L there,* [she anxiously wrote Ozias M. Hatch,] *will*
> *you say to him, that our* dear little Taddie, *is quite sick.*
> *The Dr thinks it might prove a* slight *attack of* lung *fever.*
> *I am feeling troubled & it would be a comfort to have him,*
> *at home. He passed a bad night, I do not like his symptoms,*
> *and will be glad, if he hurries home.*

But there is no evidence that Lincoln got back to Springfield until March 3.

He was long used to Mary's hysterical reaction to the children's illnesses. Tad recovered without his father.

On a happier occasion, in June 1859, Willie got to travel to Chicago with his father. The middle child had become quite different from his brothers. Though he was equally mischievous, he was also thoughtful and sensitive and, like his father, a talented writer, even as a young boy. From his hotel in Chicago, Willie wrote a charming letter to his friend Henry Remann, describing his trip in beautiful detail. This is how life at the busy Tremont House seemed to the wide-eyed eight-year-old:

> *This town is a very beautiful place. Me and father went to two theatres the other night. Me and father have a nice little room to ourselves. We have two little pitcher[s] on a washstand. The smallest one for me the largest one for father. We have two little towels on a top of both pitchers. The smallest one for me, the largest one for father.*
>
> *We have two little beds in the room. The smallest one for me, the largest one for father.*
>
> *We have two little wash basin[s]. The smallest one for me, the largest one for father. The weather is very very fine here in this town. Was [at] this exhibition on Wednesday before last.*

While Lincoln and Willie were enjoying Chicago, Bob was left at home to help his mother care for Tad and the household. Records show that Bob made several trips to a Springfield dry-goods store that week, buying seventeen pounds of sugar and a silk tie—probably as a reward for himself. Not until Abraham and Willie returned did Mary make her way back to the store to buy ice cream for everybody.

On a trip to Ohio later that same year, Mary and one of the younger boys—we are not sure which—got to accompany Lincoln on a speaking tour. They visited with a Todd cousin in Cincinnati and then traveled on to Indiana for another round of speeches. Excited Republican audiences cheered Lincoln wherever he appeared. Local newspapers even began suggesting him as a possible candidate for national office the following year. Mary, of course, was thrilled to bask in her

Abraham Lincoln and his son Willie stayed at this first-class Chicago hotel—the Tremont House—when they visited the city in 1859.

husband's new success. "*Words* cannot express what a merry time, we had," she wrote to a friend after their Ohio trip.

But Mary had more reason than ever to feel lonely when they returned home, particularly once Lincoln resumed his demanding schedule, both in Springfield and on the road. Something was radically different in the Lincoln household. It suddenly seemed emptier than ever. Robert had left for school.

With much excitement, sixteen-year-old Bob had gone east to Boston to take an entrance test for admission to Harvard College. But a year's recent schooling at a small Springfield academy with a very grand name—Illinois State University— had hardly prepared him for the country's most famous college. As Bob later admitted about his time at Illinois State: "we did just what pleased us," with "study consuming only a very small portion of time." Bob failed the Harvard entrance exam.

Meanwhile, Willie and Tad began attending the same Springfield school where their oldest brother had started his education: Miss Corcoran's Academy. Willie took to his work, but Tad had difficulty learning. He had a lisp and a speech disorder and had trouble paying attention. Today, doctors might give such children medication to help calm them down. But no such drugs existed in the 1850s, though Tad's parents did not seem terribly upset that he did little work at school. Today Tad might be diagnosed as "learning disabled," but 150 years ago his parents simply concluded that he was high-spirited.

Lincoln and Mary always expected more from their firstborn. After Bob failed the Harvard tests, his parents decided to enroll him at the Phillips Exeter Academy, a well-respected prep school in faraway New Hampshire that specialized in getting its students ready for Harvard. Mary missed Bob enormously. "I am feeling quite lonely, as *Bob*, left" for the northeast, Mary confided to a friend. "[I]t almost appears, as if light & mirth, had departed with him. I will not see him for ten months." After a separation of nearly a year, she admitted that "at times I feel *wild* to see him."

She hinted that with her eldest son away, she preferred traveling with her husband rather than staying home with her little ones. "I miss Bob, so much," Mary confessed to a friend, "that I do not feel settled down, as much as I used to & find myself going on trips quite frequently." She made plans to take Bob to visit the White Mountains in New England the following summer. But the trip never came off. Late in the summer of 1860, Bob passed his Harvard admission tests on his second try and made plans to go to college.

Back home, Lincoln lavished whatever attention he could spare on young Willie and Tad, but with his mind often wandering, the busy politician could not always take the time needed to deal successfully with their needs. Once, when the boys burst into loud and prolonged sobbing at a local drugstore, the owner asked Lincoln what was wrong. "Just what's the matter with the whole world," came the tired reply. "I've got three walnuts and each of them wants two." It often seemed to Lincoln that he did not have enough so-called walnuts to give to his very demanding boys—either financially or in fatherly attention.

Cooper Union was a new co-ed college in New York City when Lincoln arrived in February 1860 to deliver "the speech that made him President."

CHAPTER SEVEN
Father Runs for President

Bob was enjoying life at Phillips Exeter Academy, though he was forever asking his father to send him money—not unlike today's students. A classmate remembered Bob as "a neat-looking boy, a favorite in the school and popular with the girls." Whether he missed his family, no one is sure.

But in 1859, an unexpected opportunity arose that would bring son and father together again for an unforgettable reunion. That October, a group of young New York Republicans invited Lincoln to give a major speech in Brooklyn. His hosts hoped the westerner could appeal to an eastern audience—and thus become a stronger possibility for the presidential nomination the following spring.

Lincoln accepted the invitation but delayed his trip until late February 1860. He had never before spoken in the New York area, and he wanted extra time to compose a perfect address for this crucial occasion. He even bought a new suit for the trip.

The journey east took three exhausting days, and not until Lincoln arrived at his New York hotel did he learn that his speech had been moved from a Brooklyn church to a brand-new Manhattan college. It was called Cooper Union. Determined to succeed, Lincoln worked further on his oration. Then, on February 27, 1860, he delivered a masterpiece to 1,200 cheering men and women gathered in the college auditorium. "Let us have faith," he ended his speech, "that right makes might." The hope of freedom was sure to defeat the evil of slavery.

Newspapers promptly reprinted the speech, hailing it as a great triumph for Lincoln. Editors described him as far more dignified than the prairie debater they had read about. Suddenly, the man who had lost the Senate election to the Democrat Douglas was being seriously discussed as the next Republican nominee for president.

Just hours before speaking at Cooper Union—on the morning of February 27, 1860—Lincoln posed for this photograph at Mathew Brady's studio on Broadway. It became so popular that Lincoln later admitted the speech and picture "made me President."

Always planning to detour north to visit his boy, Lincoln must have been thrilled when he received additional invitations to give speeches in Connecticut, Rhode Island, and New Hampshire. Ever eager to win more support, he was pleased to learn that he would be able to combine business and pleasure. He had not seen Bob for months. But the day before, New Hampshire Republicans had sent him an urgent telegram: "Will you speak to the Republicans of Exeter when you arrive here. And what night. Please answer by telegraph." Lincoln accepted the fact that his trip to his son's new hometown would be not only personal but political.

After another speech in Connecticut, Lincoln boarded a morning train to Exeter. Nearly six hours later, at 4:27 p.m. on Wednesday, February 29, he arrived in the New Hampshire village where Bob went to school. If he was not in class, the young man surely greeted his father at the platform. But it was not to be an exclusively private hello. Before he even left the depot, Lincoln was surrounded by a group of local Republicans wondering if he would deliver additional speeches in nearby towns. As usual, Bob had to share his father with others. Still, Bob Lincoln always liked to believe that his father came to Exeter primarily "to see how I was getting along."

The answer was: surprisingly well. The lad was showing real promise in his studies at Phillips Exeter Academy. His test scores were good. At the time of his father's visit, he was earning 8s and 9s in Latin, 7s and 8s in Greek, and mostly 9s in math, on a scale of 1 to 10. Teachers based grades on recitation, composition, and scholarship. Bob would finish his first term with an excellent 8.9 average— much higher than the 6.5 earned by his best friend and roommate at school, George Clayton Latham (his pal since their days together back at Illinois State University).

By his second and third terms, Bob would further improve to 9s and 10s. Lincoln was pleased to learn of Robert's success; after all, he was paying all of twenty-four dollars per year for the boy's education, not counting two dollars weekly for room and board. Lights and fuel cost twenty-five cents extra! None of Lincoln's letters to his son from that period survives—the ever-shy Bob likely destroyed them years later. But there can be little doubt that his father pressured him to succeed when Bob tried out again for Harvard. Bob's roommate, George, had failed on his first try, too, and since George's own father was dead, Lincoln took it

Robert T. Lincoln as he looked as a student around 1860, the year his father paid him a visit at Phillips Exeter Academy in New Hampshire. Though Mary missed Robert deeply, she later claimed "it was a great relief to us all, when he was sent East to school."

upon himself to write a note trying to give his son's good friend more confidence.

For his letter to George Latham, Lincoln chose words that he must have used to encourage his own boy as well: "I have scarcely felt greater pain in my life than on learning . . . that you had failed to enter Harvard University. And yet there is very little in it, if you will allow no feeling of *discouragement* to seize, and prey upon you. It is a *certain* truth that you *can* enter, and graduate in, Harvard University; and having made the attempt, you *must* succeed in it. '*Must*' is the word." Perhaps inspired by his friend's famous father, George eventually made it to college after all—but to Yale, not Harvard.

Like many other Exeter students, Bob and George were allowed to live off campus as long as they honored a 7:00 p.m. curfew. They roomed together at Mr. and Mrs. Samuel B. Clarke's brick home on Hemlock Square. But during his visit, Lincoln probably lodged elsewhere.

Early on the morning of March 1, Lincoln boarded the 7:00 a.m. train for nearby Concord, New Hampshire, where he gave a speech at 1:30 p.m. This time, at last, Bob got to travel along with him, as did friend George. The boy had last seen his father perform in a debate with Douglas at Alton, Illinois, more than a year earlier. The local Republican newspapers seemed impressed by the politician from faraway Illinois. One declared: "He displays more shrewdness, more knowledge of the masses of mankind than any other public speaker we have heard."

His success growing, Lincoln headed back to Exeter, where he deposited Bob and George, then headed off to nearby Dover, about eighteen miles to the north. Lincoln had been officially invited there by the town's Republican chairman, who had sent the invitation not to Lincoln but to his son. The note asked Bob to inquire whether his father could be "persuaded to deliver an address upon political topics before the citizens of this city." Bob very properly replied that he would give his father the message when he could, and promised: "he will answer it for himself, though I have no doubt he will be happy to comply with your kind invitation should his time permit." It was a very mature letter for a sixteen-year-old. And Bob was certainly correct about how his father would respond to the invitation. Lincoln accepted, of course, and off he went yet again.

Not until Saturday, March 3, did Lincoln finally return to Exeter to resume his so-called reunion with Bob. But once more, the boy would be forced to share his father with hundreds of others. After three more New Hampshire engagements,

Lincoln was finally scheduled to face his son's classmates and teachers—not to mention Bob himself—with a speech near the school.

This time, the crowd was so thick outside Exeter's Young Men's Working Club that even the speaker's son had to push his way into the building. When Lincoln finally entered from the rear of the hall, one of Bob's school friends, Robert Atkins, took one look at the tall, gangly guest of honor and thought: "What a darned fool I've been to walk up here through the mud to hear *that* man speak." Within ten minutes, however, he admitted: "I was glad I was there."

Marshall Snow, another of Bob's Exeter chums, attended Lincoln's talk, too. Like most of his classmates, he liked Bob Lincoln. He thought him a "very good dresser" and now was curious to see what his famous father looked like. Would he be as dapper as his son? When the speaker arrived on stage and "succeeded in arranging his long legs under or about" his chair, it was clear that the older Lincoln did not much resemble the younger one. As a surprised Snow described the speaker: "His hair was rumpled, his neckwear was all awry, he sat somewhat bent in the chair, and altogether presented a very remarkable, and, to us, disappointing appearance."

"We sat and stared at Mr. Lincoln. We whispered to each other: 'Isn't it too bad Bob's father is so homely? Don't you feel sorry for him?'"

But when Lincoln "untangled those long legs," drew himself up to his full height, and launched into his speech, "not ten minutes had passed . . . before his uncouth appearance was absolutely forgotten by us boys. . . . His face lighted up and the man was changed; it seemed absolutely like another person speaking to us. . . . There was no more pity for our friend Bob; we were proud of his father."

The speeches behind him, Abraham Lincoln finally rested, visited with Bob, but complained about the lack of news from home. As always, he seemed more worried about Willie and Tad than about their older brother.

The truth was, Lincoln was irritated because he had received no letters from his wife during his travels. He became particularly worried when Bob told him his younger brothers had come down with an illness after his father had departed. Lincoln sat down to write a long letter to Mary (see page 72) describing his speeches at Cooper Union and after. He seemed glad to be with Bob—but also eager to get back to Illinois.

Exeter, N. H. March 4. 1860
Dear Wife:

When I wrote you before [a letter that has since vanished] *I was just starting out on a little speech-making tour, taking the boys with me. On Thursday they went with me to Concord, where I spoke in day-light. and back to Manchester, where I spoke at night. Friday we came down to Lawrence— the place of the Pemberton Mill tragedy—where we remained four hours awaiting the train back to Exeter. When it came, we went upon it to Exeter where the boys got off, and I went on to Dover and spoke there Friday evening. Saturday I came back to Exeter, reaching here about noon, and finding the boys all right, having caught up with their lessons. Bob had a letter from you saying Willie and Taddy were very sick the Saturday after I left. Having no despatch from you, and having one from Springfield, of Wednesday, from Mr. [Harrison G.] Fitzhugh, saying nothing about our family, I trust the dear little fellows are well again.*

This is Sunday morning: and according to Bob's orders, I am to go to church once to-day. Tomorrow I bid farewell to the boys, go to Hartford, Conn. and speak there in the evening; Tuesday at Meriden, Wednesday at New-Haven—and Thursday at Woonsocket R. I. Then I start home, and I think I will not stop. I may be delayed in New-York City an hour or two. I have been unable to escape this toil. If I had foreseen it I think I would not have come East at all. The speech at New-York, being within my calculation before I started, went off passably well, and gave me no trouble whatever. The difficulty was to make nine others, before reading audiences, who have already seen all my ideas in print.

If the trains do not lie over Sunday, of which I do not know, I hope to be home to-morrow week. Once started I shall come as quick as possible.

Kiss the dear boys for Father

Affectionately
A. Lincoln

The only satisfaction the weary politician found that day came with the receipt of a letter sent "care of Robert T. Lincoln, Exeter Academy" by his Cooper Union hosts. Inside was a check for two hundred dollars, Lincoln's fee for his New York speech. "I would that it were $200,000," wrote his grateful host, "for you are worthy of it. You 'hit the nail on the head' here; & long, very long will your speech be remembered in this City."

Then, just as Robert had "ordered," it was off to Sunday worship services at the Second Congregational Church. That evening, some of Bob's friends came to call at his lodgings to meet his famous father, among them a young student named Robert Cluskey.

"Cluskey plays the banjo," Bob announced to his father.

"Does he?" Lincoln replied enthusiastically. Then he asked the boy, "Where is your banjo?"

"It is at my room," Cluskey answered.

"Can't you get it?"

"Oh, I don't think you would care for it, Mr. Lincoln."

"Oh, yes."

So Cluskey went home and got his banjo, returned, and played a few tunes for Bob's delighted father. At one point, Lincoln impulsively turned to his son and declared: "Robert, you ought to have one." Bob may have felt embarrassed—as he so often did—by his father's informal behavior.

No one knows how long the little concert continued or how late father and son stayed awake that Sunday night. But at seven the next morning, Lincoln made his farewells and dutifully dragged himself to the Exeter depot for the train that would take him to Connecticut—and yet more speeches. The next time he saw Bob he was the Republican candidate for the presidency. And they would never have so close a relationship again.

Few people truly expected Lincoln to win the nomination when the Republican Convention began in Chicago that May. Despite his triumphs in the East, the Springfield lawyer remained a dark horse. Several better-known politicians were favored to win more consideration for the top prize.

Lincoln did not go to the convention himself. Instead, he stayed in Springfield. To calm his nerves, he played handball with friends while the ballots were being counted hundreds of miles to the north. Before long, the astonishing news flashed throughout the town: Abraham Lincoln had been nominated for president on the third ballot. Exuberant, Lincoln rushed home to tell his family. Mary quickly made sure that Willie and Tad got two of the little flags that the delegates had waved for Lincoln at the Chicago convention. The boys, she wrote, were "urgent to have" them.

Before long, Lincoln was not only the Republican nominee; he was the favorite to win the White House in the fall—even though he was by far the least famous man running for president. That was because the opposition Democrats could not agree on a nominee of their own. They soon split into separate Northern and Southern parties and chose two different leaders to oppose the Republican from Illinois. His Northern Democratic opponent would be none other than Stephen A. Douglas, climaxing their twenty years of rivalry. But it would not be a close contest. When a fourth presidential candidate was chosen to run as well, few experts doubted that Lincoln would emerge the victor in November.

That summer, Lincoln did no public campaigning of his own. In those days, presidential candidates were expected to remain silent and close to home. For the first time in years, he stayed quietly in Springfield and made none of his famous speeches. Yet if Mary believed that her husband's new status would bring him closer to the family, she soon learned otherwise. Lincoln grew busier than ever, even if he now worked only a few blocks away, at a new office suite inside the state capitol building. "This summer, we have had . . . no time to be occupied, with home affairs," she complained during the campaign.

Close as he stayed to home, Lincoln remained completely focused on the race for the White House. He had many people to see and endless letters to write to supporters all over the country. Though he did not "appear" at campaign rallies, he did allow photographers and painters to pose him for a number of new pictures. Why did this modest man suddenly allow his face to be copied by so many artists? The explanation was simple: to help him win the election. Voters had heard disturbing reports about Lincoln's homeliness. Some actually feared he was simply too ugly to be president. The new images were meant to show a pleasant-looking and dignified Abraham Lincoln.

Thomas Hicks, the first artist to arrive in town for such an effort, nearly failed in the attempt. It was not Lincoln who made the project difficult but, as usual, his unpredictable, uncontrollable boys. The New York painter set up his canvas on an

Candidate Lincoln posed for this Thomas Hicks painting in Springfield in June 1860. The Republican nominee for president told the artist he thought the portrait had a "somewhat pleasanter expression than I usually have."

easel in Lincoln's office and began his portrait. Things went smoothly—that is, until the Lincoln boys intruded onto the scene.

While Lincoln was posing, Tad and a "companion"—probably none other than his older brother Willie—stole "noiselessly into the office. His father was sitting at his desk with his back to them, and so absorbed that he did not hear them come in. I was busy with the portrait."

Hicks had left his full tubes of gooey paint open on a nearby table. Naturally, the boys began squeezing some bright red onto their palms and proceeded to spread it onto the wall. Next they took "the brightest blue" and "smeared that in another place, and afterward they smeared the yellow."

"I saw their excitement and mischief from the beginning," the artist remembered, "but held my peace and enjoyed watching the enthusiastic young colorists, as they made their first effort in brilliant wall decoration." The Lincoln boys had struck again—"as still as mice" as they smeared fresh oil paint "all over their hands, their faces, and their clothes," and the office of the Republican candidate for president of the United States.

Once Lincoln finally realized that something was happening behind him, he abruptly turned around in his chair. Artist Hicks probably expected his subject to spank or at least scold the children. Naturally, he did neither. Lincoln merely said, in "the mildest tone and with the greatest affection, 'Boys! Boys! You mustn't meddle with Mr. Hicks's paints; now run home and have your faces and hands washed.'" And as Thomas Hicks recalled with amazement, "the little fellows took his advice and left the office without a word."

Tad and Willie thoroughly enjoyed the attention the campaign brought to their father, the entire town—and, of course, themselves. They excitedly watched a big parade march past their house, sang along with the new campaign songs written in their father's honor (such as "Old Abe Lincoln Came Out of the Wilderness"), and waved each new picture of Lincoln like tiny voters at an election rally. Once, when his father was posing for another painter, Tad burst into the office, running "everywhere at once, being repeatedly recaptured by his mother." But not before the boy spotted the newest painting. He quickly shouted to a pal: "Come here, Jim; here's another Old Abe."

"Old Abe" was the nation's new informal nickname for the Republican candidate for president. Mary considered it rude and undignified. But Lincoln did

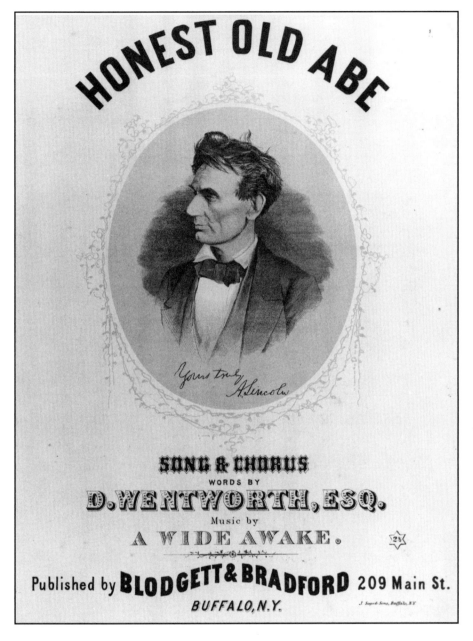

Campaign music of 1860 celebrated Lincoln's personal traits. This sheet-music cover emphasized his already legendary honesty. The portrait was based on a three-year-old photo that Mary disliked because of the "wild" hair (see page 42).

not mind when his youngest son used it. "Did you hear that?" he asked the artist. "He got that on the street, I suppose." The painter observed "with what interested pride Lincoln's eyes followed" Tad "about the room," wherever his little legs took him.

On yet another occasion that same summer, Willie and Tad got to pose with their father for a different kind of campaign picture—this one a photograph of the

Another example of 1860 campaign music featured small images of young
Abraham Lincoln as a railsplitter and flatboatman. Pictures that stressed
the candidate's virtues sidestepped controversial issues like slavery.

nominee standing in the front yard of the family home. As photographer John Adams Whipple aimed his camera from across the street, Lincoln and Willie firmly clutched the front fence for the lengthy exposure, trying hard not to move. It took up to fifteen seconds to make a photo, and subjects posing for the camera had to hold very still. But of course, Tad could not do so—or simply did not want to try. The final picture (see page 91) showed the house beautifully and included the unmistakable figure of tall Abraham Lincoln and a little boy next to him, wearing a cap. This was Willie. But Tad, half-hiding mischievously behind a corner gate post, must have wriggled too much. All one sees of him is a blur.

Back in New Hampshire, Bob loyally joined the local Republican marching club known as "Wide Awakes." They wore special hats and oil slickers and carried fire-lit torches in nighttime Lincoln parades. Dutifully, Bob joined in at several rallies and shouted himself hoarse for the Republican candidate who happened to be his father. Somehow he also managed to study hard and pass his entrance exams for college. Writing to a friend that summer, his father proudly announced: "Our eldest boy, Bob, has been away from us nearly a year at school, and will enter Harvard University this month. He promises very well, considering we never controlled him much." Even when he was complimenting Bob, Lincoln always seemed to add a small insult, too.

But in Springfield, the ever-busy Lincoln made every attempt to steal precious moments with his two younger sons, from whom he expected so little in return. A local editor found him at home one day, alone with Willie and Tad, happily playing at spinning a top—"having a little season of relaxation with the boys." Another visitor glimpsed him lying on the parlor floor, absorbed in reading a newspaper while his small sons climbed over him and happily jumped on his legs. Willie suffered a dangerous bout of scarlet fever that summer, and for a time the Lincolns worried that he was in danger of dying, like his brother Eddy. But he recovered, and visitors soon saw him running barefoot about the Lincoln home, as full of energy as before.

Through all the tense months of the campaign, Lincoln did his best to keep calm. But as usual, Mary found relaxation impossible. For a time, in fact, she appeared to be much more worried about the election than her husband was. "I scarcely know, how I would bear up, under defeat," she admitted. But this was one loss she would never have to face.

This 1860 election poster showed Lincoln (left) and his vice presidential running mate, Hannibal Hamlin of Maine, arranged beneath an inspiring symbol of patriotism: an American eagle.

CHAPTER EIGHT
President-Elect Lincoln and Family

On November 6, 1860, America's voters spoke. Although he received almost no support in the South, Lincoln easily won the election for president by sweeping to victory in every Northern state except New Jersey. All of the states where he had toured and given speeches during his wintertime visit to both Cooper Union and his son Bob voted strongly for Lincoln.

Still, when all the ballots were counted, Lincoln had earned less than 40 percent nationally. In total, three out of every five voters had cast their ballots *against* Lincoln. Deeply divided, the country grew uneasy with the result. Worried that they had chosen the wrong leader, some Northerners suggested that Lincoln was not up to the job after all. Meanwhile, fearful he would act to end slavery, angry Southern leaders began talking openly of splitting away from the United States altogether and forming a country of their own.

Two weeks later, while the Lincolns prepared for Springfield's official celebration of his victory, a crowd of proud neighbors swarmed outside the Lincoln home to congratulate him. Every time the crowd let out a cheer, Willie and Tad replied with "juvenile yells" of their own from the windows. Meanwhile, strangers trampled Mary's carpets, ate her food, and pointed rudely in her direction, asking each other, "Is that the old woman?" The family's life in the spotlight was getting harder to enjoy—at least for the parents.

As the country's political crisis worsened, Congress met and began considering laws that would make slavery permanent forever and even expand it to the West Coast. A Peace Convention met in the capital to explore similar compromise plans. Though opposed to any idea that would spread slavery, Lincoln enjoyed no real

**FOR PRESIDENT,
ABRAM LINCOLN.**

A Home for the Homeless.

**VICE PRESIDENT,
HANNIBAL HAMLIN.**

Many 1860 campaign images emphasized Lincoln's humble roots and capacity for hard work. Here he is again shown as a young railsplitter.

power to influence these discussions. He was not yet president. But he made clear to visitors that nothing would ever force him to agree to expanding slavery—even if it meant war.

In those days, presidential inaugurations took place long after Election Day—in March, not January as they do now. With four long months to go before he could head to Washington and take the oath of office as president, Lincoln had no choice but to wait anxiously for his term to begin. All he could do was hope that the Union would not split in two before he got the chance to lead. The famous public speaker had no choice but to remain silent, exactly as he had been during the campaign. Just as the customs of the day called for presidential candidates to say nothing publicly, tradition also required presidents-elect to be equally silent. For Lincoln, it was perhaps the most frustrating time of his career.

For Willie and Tad Lincoln, however, life was never more thrilling. Springfield swarmed with famous visitors. The many callers included famous men eager for jobs in the new administration, along with well-wishers hoping just to meet the boys' father. Crowding town, too, were artists seeking to paint new portraits, plus photographers, sculptors, and reporters. Hotels filled up, the night sky lit up with fireworks, and bands of musicians marched through the streets playing campaign tunes.

To the boys, their ever more famous father still seemed as tolerant and loving as ever, as wonderful a playmate as he always was—that is, when he could spare them his time and attention. But one thing was certain: he *looked* different. Beginning just after his election, Lincoln stopped shaving. Within weeks, he had grown his now-famous beard.

Oddly, it was a little girl, rather than his own little boys, who had suggested it. Eleven-year-old Grace Bedell from Westfield, in upstate New York, had written Lincoln in October to tell him: "I have got 4 brother's and part of them will vote for you any way and if you will let your whiskers grow I will try and get the rest of them to vote for you." Grace thought he "would look a great deal better for your face is so thin." She also wanted to know: "Have you any little girls about as large as I am if so give them my love and tell her to write to me if you cannot answer this letter." In his now-famous reply, the president-elect disappointed Grace on both latter counts. But Grace was overjoyed to get a letter from Mr. Lincoln anyway.

As an early snow fell in Westfield, Grace excitedly opened the envelope and learned that her hero had neither little girls of his own nor plans to heed her advice and begin growing a beard. As she would soon find out, Lincoln would change his mind—at least about the whiskers.

This is what Lincoln wrote:

> My *dear little Miss.*
>
> *Your very agreeable letter of the 15th. is received.*
>
> *I regret the necessity of saying I have no daughters. I have three sons—one seventeen, one nine, and one seven, years of age. They, with their mother, constitute my whole family.*
>
> *As to the whiskers, having never worn any, do you not think people would call it a piece of silly affect[at]ion if I were to begin it now?*
>
> Your very sincere well-wisher
Lincoln

Abraham Lincoln began growing his famous beard—here seen in its earliest stages, in late November 1860—in part at the suggestion of eleven-year-old Grace Bedell from Westfield, New York. She wrote to tell him his face looked too thin without whiskers.

Lincoln received not only many letters but also many gifts during the family's final months in Springfield. Admirers sent Lincoln clothes, soap, food, and other presents, and the boys occasionally helped themselves to the things their father did not want. The president-elect did not smoke, so when one generous supporter shipped him a box of cigars, Lincoln left them at home untouched. That proved a mistake. Willie, Tad, and a neighbor boy got hold of them and snuck them off to the barn behind the Lincoln home, where they lit up. After just a few puffs from the cigars, the children became so nauseated and dizzy that they staggered out of the barn crying for help. Mary did all she could to help them recover. A neighbor remembered that their mother sympathized with them and never scolded them for either stealing or smoking.

On another occasion, Lincoln was opening his mail while posing for a new clay statuette at the St. Nicholas Hotel. Among the day's deliveries, he found a strange-looking package. It was wrapped in plain brown paper, loosely tied with string, and had no return address on it. Both Lincoln and sculptor Thomas D. Jones feared it might actually contain a bomb. At the time, Lincoln had been receiving so many violent threats to his life that their concern was entirely understandable. So Lincoln and the artist decided to open the package while pressing it up against the clay model of the president-elect's head. If it was an explosive, they reasoned, the statue would perhaps absorb the shock. But there was nothing dangerous inside the wrapping after all. Instead, Lincoln found an innocent and peculiar gift: a handmade whistle fashioned from the tail of a pig.

Entranced by the instrument, Lincoln spent the rest of the day trying to make it play music. But as hard as he blew into it, nothing came out but air. Then Tad discovered the whistle and had no trouble at all making it sing—as loud as he could. Calling at the Lincoln home that evening, sculptor Jones found Tad there, "making the house vocal, if not musical, with the pig-tail whistle, blowing blasts" that rocked the whole household and the surrounding neighborhood.

Around this time, newspapers began writing often about Willie and Tad, and soon all of America knew the Lincoln boys. Isolated far away at his New Hampshire school, Bob may have grown a bit jealous. If so, it was understandable. Though he was becoming something of a snob and liked his privacy and independence, he may have missed the limelight a bit.

Writing to his mother in December, he reported that he was "back at Exeter," where he felt "very much at home"—

While posing for this statuette in Springfield in late January 1861, Lincoln found a mysterious, loosely tied package in his morning mail. It turned out that the package contained a harmless gift—a homemade pig-tail whistle. The Lincolns later displayed a copy of the bust in the Red Room of the White House.

words that probably hurt Mary's feelings. Bob had just learned that his parents had traveled to Chicago a few weeks after Election Day, where large crowds had made a great fuss over them. "Aint you *beginning* to get a little tired of this constant uproar?" he pompously asked his mother. Bob, too, had recently been asked to make a speech—by "a fellow who is boring me considerably," he reported. He "must be the biggest fool in the world," Bob declared, to imagine that Bob would ever agree to deliver a political talk in public before "a vast sea of human faces." It was almost as if Bob were declaring his father's profession to be undignified, even unworthy. Whether his parents liked it or not, Bob was becoming his own person.

Robert Lincoln as he looked in 1861—the period when he first became known as "The Prince of Rails."

After all, Mary explained, her eldest son was just seventeen.

The teenager did travel home to Springfield for Christmas but once again found politics crowding into family time—but it was now marked by a ferocious public anger he had never witnessed in the past. That very holiday week, the state of South Carolina seceded from the Union. The worst crisis in American history was truly underway. A group of so-called South Carolina Palmetto Boys then sent the president-elect a copy of their state's printed secession proclamation, marked up with a handwritten, somewhat threatening inscription. Bob was distressed to find it lying about at home. Patting his son's head, Lincoln tried to reassure the worried young man by joking that "it must have been intended for a Christmas gift." Meanwhile, the youngsters hungrily opened their Christmas stockings, bulging with traditional gifts, as if everything in the country were back to normal for the holiday. Of course, it was not.

In January 1861, Mary nevertheless decided that she must journey to New York to buy new clothes and accessories for her new life in Washington. Bob accompanied his mother on the trip. Along the way, he found that fame brought both opportunities and embarrassment. On the positive side, New Yorkers gave the young man special tours of attractions like the stock exchange and other sites designed "to please the young gentleman from the Far West." But Mary lost her temper in public from time to time during the vacation, and Bob was mortified. On the way home, his mother became especially furious when a railroad conductor in Buffalo refused her a free ticket. Bob was forced to warn the ticket agent: "The Old Lady is raising hell about her passes."

Returning home to Springfield, the president-elect's son resumed his school vacation saddled with a funny new title of his own. Queen Victoria's son, the Prince of Wales, had recently toured America. He had even stopped briefly at Springfield, though Lincoln had refused to go down to the railroad depot to greet him, thinking it would look undignified. Americans at the time tended to think of Lincoln as a man of the people, and many called him "The Railsplitter," because as a young boy on the frontier he had once split wooden rails to make fences. Now reporters combined these "titles"—one describing English royalty, the other describing a self-made American—and created a new nickname for Robert Todd Lincoln: not the Prince of Wales but "The Prince of *Rails*." Supposedly, his mother did not like it.

But fame brought Bob new attention where he wanted it most. The once-shy seventeen-year-old suddenly seemed to dazzle the local girls with "the improving influences of genteel, well dressed and well behaved Boston," wrote one reporter. Of course, his father's new celebrity did not harm his popularity.

The reporter saw the "heir apparent" walking the streets with his father, "bringing up the rear of the 'old man,'" and looking even more dignified than his father. Lincoln still appeared, to Robert's dismay, as if he had slept in his black suit, which did not fit him properly in the first place. The journalist could not help noticing how different the two looked. Bob's elegance, he wrote, was "a striking contrast to the loose, careless, awkward rigging of his Presidential father." Another observer praised Bob as "a young man of . . . much dignity" and "a dutiful and affectionate son." Bob no doubt enjoyed the benefits his father's celebrity status brought his way—especially his new popularity with neighbor girls who used to call him "cockeye" before his surgery. But he came to hate the press coverage he started receiving. From 1860 on, Bob was suspicious of newspapermen and embarrassed about publicity.

Willie and Tad were too young to mind the attention. If anything, they rejoiced in it. They rushed into their father's statehouse office at will and chatted amiably with the strangers waiting on long lines to visit him, many of whom greedily hungered for federal jobs. (Some office seekers, as they were called, took to writing to Bob in an effort to get his father's attention.) One visitor who dined at the Lincoln home during the period that became known as the "winter of secession" was distracted to observe Willie and Tad climbing all over their father, standing on his boots, and sticking their fingers in his eyes, nose, and ears. Not once did Lincoln interrupt the flow of his conversation. He continued talking to his astonished visitor as if nothing else were happening.

The younger boys were probably saddened for a while when their parents began packing their belongings for the move to Washington. But they were likely so excited about the upcoming train journey—and the future prospect of living in the famous White House—that they had no time to be upset.

Except, that is, over one particular decision. During their brief lifetimes, their parents had seldom said no to any request or demand that Willie and Tad issued. But when the boys begged Lincoln to let them take their dog, Fido, with the family to Washington, he simply would not grant their request. The trip was much too

The Lincolns left their family pet, Fido, behind in Springfield when they headed to the White House in February 1861. The dog was taken to the local photographer's studio in Springfield for this keepsake. The Lincoln boys took this very copy to Washington.

long, he told the heartbroken boys. Fido would never survive the journey. Instead the Lincolns gave the large golden dog to a neighbor and even included one of the horsehair sofas on which Fido enjoyed sleeping. To create a souvenir, the Lincolns took the dog to a photo gallery to have his portrait made. If the boys could not take their pet to the White House, at least they would have as a keepsake their own photograph of the dog they were forced to leave behind. (Years later, like his famous master, Fido was "assassinated"—stabbed to death on a Springfield street by an angry drunk.)

On February 6, 1861, Abraham and Mary Lincoln hosted a farewell party at their Springfield home to say a final good-bye to their friends and neighbors. It was difficult to celebrate the past without thinking of the perilous future. The political

The Lincolns were not the only "First Family" in America in 1861. Around the same time, Jefferson Davis took the oath of office as president of the Confederate States of America. In this print, issued years after the war, are pictured from left to right: daughter Maggie Hayes; grandson Jefferson Hayes; Davis; daughter Winnie; and wife, Varina Davis.

crisis had grown much worse. Six more states had joined South Carolina and quit the Union. Now they had formed their own country—which they named the Confederate States of America. They had even chosen a president of their own, Jefferson Davis of Mississippi. The country really had divided into two, North and South. Still, Lincoln showed no signs of backing down on the slavery issue.

Despite these upsetting developments, "hundreds of well dressed ladies and gentlemen gathered" at the home on Eighth and Jackson streets in Springfield for the Lincolns' farewell reception. The house grew so crowded that some guests had to wait twenty minutes just to get through the front door. Willie and Tad observed the event merrily, causing havoc wherever and whenever they could and earning

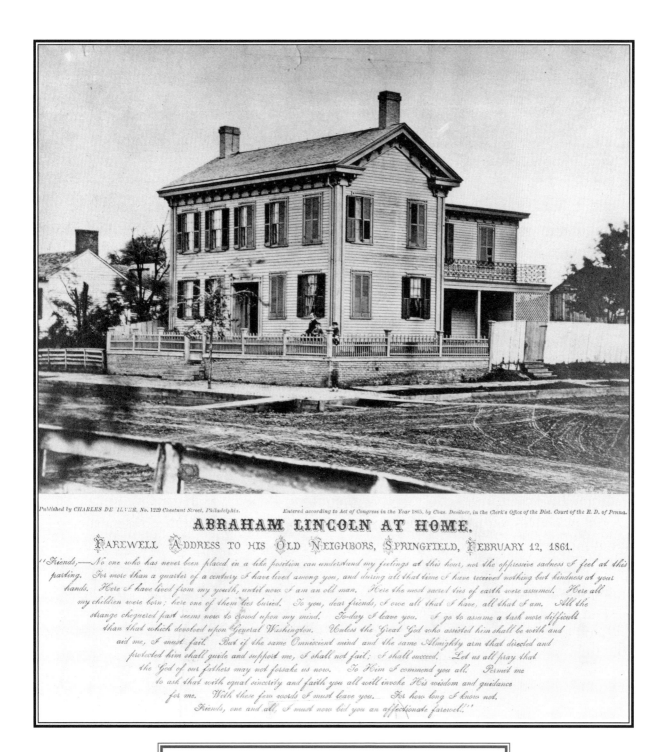

Published by CHARLES DE ILVER, No. 1229 Chestnut Street, Philadelphia.   Entered according to Act of Congress in the Year 1865, by Chas. Desilver, in the Clerk's Office of the Dist. Court of the E. D. of Penna.

ABRAHAM LINCOLN AT HOME.

FAREWELL ADDRESS TO HIS OLD NEIGHBORS, SPRINGFIELD, FEBRUARY 12, 1861.

"Friends,——No one who has never been placed in a like position can understand my feelings at this hour, nor the oppressive sadness I feel at this parting. For more than a quarter of a century I have lived among you, and during all that time I have received nothing but kindness at your hands. Here I have lived from my youth, until now I am an old man. Here the most sacred ties of earth were assumed. Here all my children were born; here one of them lies buried. To you, dear friends, I owe all that I have, all that I am. All the strange chequered past seems now to crowd upon my mind. To-day I leave you. I go to assume a task more difficult than that which devolved upon General Washington. Unless the Great God who assisted him shall be with and aid me, I must fail. But if the same Omniscient mind and the same Almighty arm that directed and protected him shall guide and support me, I shall not fail; I shall succeed. Let us all pray that the God of our fathers may not forsake us now. To Him I commend you all. Permit me to ask that with equal sincerity and faith you all will invoke His wisdom and guidance for me. With these few words I must leave you. For how long I know not. Friends, one and all, I must now bid you an affectionate farewell."

This photograph celebrates Lincoln's farewell to his neighbors in February 1861, but it was actually taken a year earlier. Lincoln is seen with his boys Willie and Tad. Little Tad squirmed too much as the picture was being taken and appears as little more than a blur. Note the muddy streets and wooden curb planks.

no reprimand from their parents, as usual. But when Bob managed to squeeze himself into the receiving line in the parlor, he had far worse luck trying to amuse his parents. Attempting a little joke, Bob greeted his father as if he were a stranger. "Good evening *Mr. Lincoln!*" he announced gravely. For this, in front of all the guests, "his father gave him a gentle slap in the face." Lincoln and his eldest son were clearly becoming strangers to each other.

Bob later admitted rather sadly: "During my childhood and early youth, my father was constantly away from home attending to his law practice and making political speeches. When he became president, I went away to [prep] school and afterward to Harvard College. Henceforth any intimacy between us became impossible." Bob believed that during the Civil War, the White House was not a home at all—but rather, as he later described it, a "gilded prison."

In early February, the Lincoln family left their house on Eighth and Jackson streets forever. The president-elect rented it to a railroad official and moved his brood into a nearby hotel until they were ready to depart Springfield. Just before the family left for Washington, Mary took the boys to Preston Butler's Springfield photo gallery and posed with them for the first and only picture ever to show them together. Bob was not included.

Against a fake backdrop that made it look as if they were standing outdoors, rather than inside a gallery, Mary wore a bonnet and shawl. Willie slipped his hand inside his jacket in an effort to look important. Looking as defiant as ever, little Tad placed his left hand on his hip and with his right hand clutched his mother— or did his mother clutch Tad's hand to keep him still? It was hard to tell.

Such details did not matter to the public. A popular illustrated newspaper soon published a large drawing of the photo, making the family more famous than ever. They would soon become even more so.

Mary posed with sons Willie (left) and Tad soon after the 1860 presidential election. It was the first—and last—time she had her picture taken with the boys. Many Americans got to see this picture—it was copied for the newspapers.

Elmer E. Ellsworth, a young law student, was a bodyguard who traveled with the Lincolns from Springfield to Washington. Ellsworth was already famous as leader of a marching unit that performed at military parades.

CHAPTER NINE
On to Washington

As much as Mary begged and pleaded, Lincoln insisted that the family could not begin their exciting voyage to Washington together.

So many threats to his life had poured into Springfield. And thousands of people were expected to greet—or perhaps menace—Lincoln along the journey. Lincoln's advisers worried that it was too dangerous for Mary and the youngest boys to leave town with the president-elect. It would be far safer for them to quietly join him the next morning. Bob alone would accompany his father out of Springfield.

Of course, they would not travel completely alone—anything but. Throughout the long inaugural journey, Lincoln would be well protected by the largest and strongest security force ever gathered to guard an incoming president.

Longtime friend and fellow lawyer Ward Hill Lamon, who was nearly as tall as Lincoln and much wider, would serve as a personal bodyguard. Young Ephraim Elmer Ellsworth would go along, too. Ellsworth, a law student in the Lincoln & Herndon office, had recently won fame as the leader of a cadet corps that performed precision marching drills. They dressed in colorful Zouave uniforms—including baggy red pants, brightly colored blue vests, and hats adorned with braided gold tassels—in imitation of the soldiers in the French Foreign Legion. Ellsworth was a particular favorite of Lincoln's, and no doubt the president-elect was glad to have him along.

To provide extra security, a number of military officers, among them future Civil War generals, joined the traveling party, too. And Mary's brother-in-law Dr. William Wallace, for whom little Willie had been named, was asked to accompany Lincoln as well—just in case the president-elect might need emergency medical attention.

Would this show of force be enough to safeguard Lincoln? Only time would tell.

Ward Hill Lamon also accompanied the Lincolns from Springfield to Washington as a bodyguard. Lamon was a burly lawyer and longtime friend who carried a knife and brass knuckles to ward off would-be attackers.

On the chilly morning of February 11, 1861, Bob and his father silently rode in a horse-drawn cart to the Springfield train station.

A light drizzle fell outside as they arrived at the little depot and strolled inside to say farewell to the close friends gathered around a warm stove. Few people spoke. No one could quite find the words to say farewell to the man who had lived among them for so long. Then, with Bob's old friend George Latham joining them for the trip, they slowly stepped outside and inched toward the tracks where their steaming train awaited them. The crowd parted as they passed by. Mary and the younger boys waved their tearful good-byes from the platform.

The group boarded the richly decorated three-car train. But just before it pulled out of Springfield, Lincoln turned one last time to the crowd from outside the caboose and removed his high silk hat. Fighting back tears, he began speaking softly but with deep emotion to the hundreds of neighbors who had braved the cold and rain to see him off. No one here had ever heard Lincoln make such a short speech—or such a personal one. Amidst total quiet—except for the sound of the raindrops and the occasional sob from a sad member of the audience—this is what he said that day:

My friends—No one, not in my situation, can appreciate my feelings of sadness at this parting. To this place, and the kindness of these people, I owe every thing. Here I have lived a quarter of a century, and have passed from a young to an old man. Here my children have been born, and one is buried. I now leave, not knowing when, or whether ever, I may return, with a task before me greater than that which faced Washington. . . . Trusting in Him, who can go with me, and remain with you and be every where for good, let us confidently hope that all will yet be well. To His care commending you, as I hope in your prayers you will commend me, I bid you an affectionate farewell.

Lincoln departed Springfield on February 11, 1861, from this small railroad depot. Here many of his closest friends gathered to say good-bye. A deeply touched Lincoln was barely able to whisper his final farewells before boarding his train and giving his last-ever speech there to a crowd of about one thousand.

And then, as the locomotive hissed a billow of white steam and sounded its loud whistle, the train slowly chugged away, taking Abraham Lincoln away forever. Old friends waved their hats and shouted good-bye until the train disappeared from view.

Just as he feared, Abraham Lincoln would never see his hometown again. Nor, for that matter, would his sons Willie and Tad.

Lincoln took these young Illinois clerks to Washington with him. John Nicolay (left) and John Hay became his White House secretaries. They later co-wrote a ten-volume book about the president. Hay became an especially good friend of Robert Lincoln's.

Later that day, the train pulled into Indianapolis, Indiana. This time the mood was joyful. With music filling the air and a vast, enthusiastic crowd on hand to welcome him, Lincoln rode off in triumph to a local hotel in a carriage pulled by four white horses. Bob and Lincoln's young private secretaries, John Nicolay and John Hay, were left to plod through the mud on foot. That night, the hotel dining room filled with admirers for a special supper in the president-elect's honor. Bob joined in the fun.

During the long dinner, Lincoln's thoughts turned to his upcoming inaugural address. He had begun working on this crucial speech weeks earlier. After composing a careful draft, he had taken his handwritten manuscript to the local Republican newspaper office in Springfield. There, he asked the editor to set it in type so it would be easier for him to read. Before leaving Springfield, Lincoln packed the newly printed speech inside a small black briefcase and entrusted it to Bob's safekeeping for the trip.

But Bob, who had been enjoying the company of the local Indianapolis girls and perhaps had been drinking too much wine as well, replied that he had no idea of the briefcase's whereabouts. As he admitted to his horrified father, he had simply handed it off to a waiter some time earlier and had no idea what had become of it.

With a "look of stupefaction" on his bearded face, Lincoln bounded downstairs toward the hotel lobby. There he leaped over the front desk, his long legs flying, and began rummaging through the huge pile of baggage that lay stacked behind it. The many black briefcases there all looked alike, so now the next president of the United States began tearing them open one by one, forcing the locks whenever he had to. He found shirt collars, a deck of cards, and a flask of whiskey in other visitors' luggage before he finally unearthed his own briefcase and clutched his lost speech with relief.

In those days, before typewriters and computers, there was no backup for such important documents. Nothing had been "saved." Had Lincoln failed to find his speech that night, he would have had no choice but to begin writing it again from scratch. He rarely lost his temper publicly, much less with his boys, but now, in front of one and all, Lincoln angrily gave Bob a piece of his mind. Then he shoved the briefcase back at him and firmly instructed his son: "Now, you keep it!" If the teenager felt humiliated by the reprimand, he did not let on. As he shrugged: "The old man might as well scold about that as something else." It is little wonder that one observer described Bob Lincoln as "probably the happiest and most carefree member of the party" heading to Washington—perhaps *too* "carefree" for his father's taste. Lincoln always expected little from Willie and Tad but seemed to demand much from their oldest brother, Bob.

The next day was Lincoln's fifty-second birthday, and his best gift turned out to be a reunion with Mary and the younger children. Their brief but nerve-racking separation at an end, the entire family now boarded a new train at Indianapolis and headed east together on the next leg of their journey. On the days that followed, they would ride through Indiana, Ohio, and across the vast Empire State. In the tiny hamlet of Westfield, Lincoln even got to meet Grace Bedell, the little girl who had suggested he grow a beard. Later, his train took the family south along the Hudson River into the biggest city in the entire country, New York, before heading off to New Jersey and Pennsylvania. In the days to come, Lincoln would be called upon to deliver dozens of speeches—from hotels, state capitols, and railroad stations—and introduce his wife and boys to the audiences that gathered to meet him.

The long voyage must have been a particular thrill for Willie. The boy had come to love studying railroad timetables. To his father's delight, Willie collected them, memorized the names of tiny, unfamiliar towns across the country, and taught himself how to pronounce them all—even the Indian names. Then he charted imaginary journeys in his mind that he hoped one day would take the family from west to east. Now, like his father, he was living his dream.

At Columbus, Ohio, sixty thousand people crowded the station to meet the presidential special and erupted into cheers when all five Lincolns emerged from their passenger car together. Lincoln lifted his hat and bowed gratefully to the crowd. The next day, as the train resumed its trip, Ward Hill Lamon entertained the passengers by playing his banjo and singing songs. Fully recovered from the mishap of the lost inaugural address, Bob happily joined in the music. His father, however, was now suffering from a sore throat. Not only was he unable to sing, but he could hardly speak above a croaking whisper. This did nothing to spoil the trip for his children. Bob was happy to meet local girls and then leave them behind each time the inaugural train left another city. Some said he drowned his sorrows with wine.

Willie and Tad made plenty of mischief of their own. At each of the brief stopovers, they would shout to the excited crowds: "Do you want to see Old Abe?" Then they would devilishly point out someone else. Wherever crowds gathered, Lincoln paused to whisper a few words of greeting to the throngs. Many of these citizens had never cast eyes on a president—much less his entire family.

Lincoln's secretary, who was not fond of all the Lincolns, was amazed at how well the family held up on the taxing journey—especially the temperamental Mary and the irrepressible youngsters. "Mrs. L. behaves quite well," John Nicolay reported to his fiancée, "—and the children have been reasonably good considering what they are."

Audiences along the way were soon demanding not only to hear from the next president but also to see his wife and their boys. On a freezing February day in Poughkeepsie, New York, Mary opened her window to wave at well-wishers, but they shouted back: "Where are the children?" Bob responded by showing his face at the window, but then someone in the crowd yelled, "Have you any more?"

But Mary simply could not get the moody Tad to make an appearance. Though he loved attention, the little one loved even more to do exactly the opposite of what his mother wanted. So as the crowd looked on and roared merrily at the comic scene, Mary tried without success "to bring a tough, rugged little fellow, about eight years of age, into sight." The more she tried to pull Tad toward the window, "the more he stubbornly persisted in throwing himself Down on the floor of the car, laughing at the fun." Finally, Mary gave up "the attempt to exhibit the 'pet of the household.'" Even the good-natured Willie was heard to say: "I wish they wouldn't stare at us so. Wasn't there ever a President who had children?"

The family did emerge back into public view together once they reached the big, crowded metropolis of New York. After riding in a long procession of carriages from the brand-new train station down Broadway to their hotel, the Astor House, Mary and Willie visited Barnum's Museum across the street. There they saw giants and giantesses, wild animals, a fat lady, and perhaps even the famous midget, Tom Thumb, who a few years later would make a special visit to the family in the White House.

Possibly they also saw the popular but racist Barnum exhibit called the "What Is It?" In truth, this pathetic "attraction" was a mentally and physically disabled African American teenager. But Barnum exhibited him as a half man–half creature from Africa. Mary and the children probably did not know that only a few months

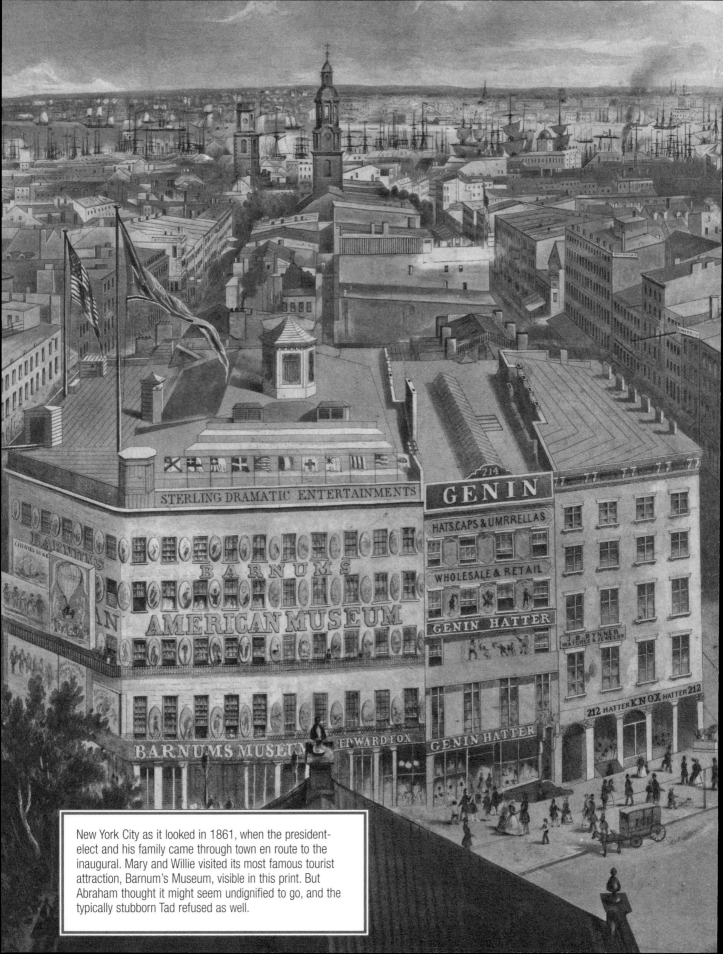

New York City as it looked in 1861, when the president-elect and his family came through town en route to the inaugural. Mary and Willie visited its most famous tourist attraction, Barnum's Museum, visible in this print. But Abraham thought it might seem undignified to go, and the typically stubborn Tad refused as well.

Cartoons of the day often showed opposition Democrats as copperhead snakes and African Americans as the "What Is It?" Even then, this sideshow attraction at Barnum's Museum was thought to be politically incorrect.

earlier, a New York cartoonist had published a comic picture showing the "What Is It?" standing alongside their own father. The vicious cartoon suggested that the Barnum attraction symbolized the future of the antislavery Republican Party. If Lincoln were to win the White House, simpleminded people like the "What Is It?" would take over the country!

Barnum invited Lincoln to his famous showplace, too, but it shocked few New Yorkers when he refused to accept. Much more surprisingly, Tad declined to go, too. The youngest Lincoln stubbornly refused to join his mother and Willie at Barnum's, arguing that he had seen "plenty of bears" back home. As always, Tad was the most unpredictable member of the family.

Lincoln did, however, go to the opera. As the audience welcomed him with loud applause, he attended a performance of a new production by Italian composer Giuseppe Verdi called *The Masked Ball*. The plot involved a scheme to assassinate an important leader. In the final act, a crowd gathers onstage wearing masks to witness the terrible murder. Perhaps advised that the story came much too close to reality, the Railsplitter did not remain to see the ending. But the Prince of Rails not only stayed behind, he actually appeared onstage himself, wearing a mask, as a "guest star" for the assassination scene. Willie and Tad got to see a stage production in New York, too. The younger children attended a play at Laura Keene's theater. They, of course, could not know it, but four years later, that same Laura Keene would be appearing onstage at another playhouse—Ford's Theatre in Washington—on the very night their father was assassinated.

Bob did not realize it at the time of his performance, but just two nights later, he played another small but key role—this time in protecting his father from a real-life murder plot that awaited him at the end of the inaugural journey. At the family's next overnight stop, in Philadelphia, a young man approached Bob at their crowded hotel and asked that he show him the way to his father's suite. Bob obliged. The stranger turned out to be Frederick Seward, son of William H. Seward, the man Lincoln had chosen to be his secretary of state. The older Seward had urgently sent his son up to Philadelphia to warn the president-elect of a genuine scheme to kill him when he reached Baltimore, Maryland.

Lincoln listened intently to Frederick's distressing report. Eventually, he decided to heed the advice. He would not appear publicly in Baltimore as scheduled. Reaching Washington alive was more important than making a public show in a hostile, proslavery city.

So after the family next visited Harrisburg, Pennsylvania, Lincoln quietly left that town along with Ward Hill Lamon and two private detectives. After racing from the governor's mansion in a horse-drawn carriage, they boarded a regularly scheduled public train, disguised as ordinary passengers, for a secret nighttime ride first to Philadelphia and then into Baltimore. Before dawn the next morning, a team of horses pulled his train across the city's deserted streets to the tracks that led to Washington. No one else on board knew that they shared the sleeping car with the next president of the United States.

This Southern city, so friendly to secession and so hostile to Lincoln, would not get to see—let alone harm—the new president. Once again, Mary and the boys were left behind to follow separately—and later on. Some witnesses reported that angry crowds did gather to shout insults at the family when they arrived in Baltimore the next morning. Mary and the boys may have been frightened by these outbursts, but if so they never let on.

President-elect Lincoln (on the flag-draped platform) raised the flag outside Independence Hall in Philadelphia on Washington's Birthday, February 22, 1861.

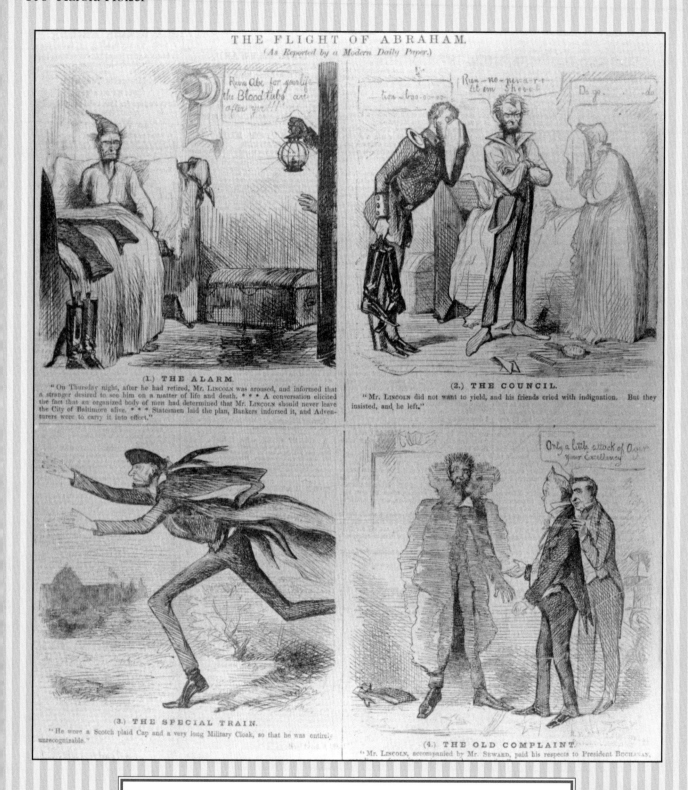

THE FLIGHT OF ABRAHAM.
(As Reported by a Modern Daily Paper.)

(1.) THE ALARM.

"On Thursday night, after he had retired, Mr. LINCOLN was aroused, and informed that a stranger desired to see him on a matter of life and death. * * * A conversation elicited the fact that an organized body of men had determined that Mr. LINCOLN should never leave the City of Baltimore alive. * * * Statesmen laid the plan, Bankers indorsed it, and Adventurers were to carry it into effect."

(2.) THE COUNCIL.

"Mr. LINCOLN did not want to yield, and his friends cried with indignation. But they insisted, and he left."

(3.) THE SPECIAL TRAIN.

"He wore a Scotch plaid Cap and a very long Military Cloak, so that he was entirely unrecognizable."

(4.) THE OLD COMPLAINT.

"Mr. LINCOLN, accompanied by Mr. SEWARD, paid his respects to President BUCHANAN.

Lincoln's secret nighttime sprint through Baltimore was arranged after he learned of death threats from that Southern city. His trip inspired many critical cartoons accusing him of cowardice. This group of drawings shows him shivering in fear and racing through the streets in disguise to avoid would-be assassins.

The danger may have been real, but political cartoonists had a field day creating exaggerated pictures that showed Lincoln as a coward, dressed in a disguise to sneak through Baltimore. Within days, the president-elect would be terribly embarrassed by his secret train ride into—and out of—Maryland. Lincoln came to think of the midnight trip as the worst mistake of his life. But at least he traveled safely—and arrived in one piece. As he told an old friend: "It ain't best to run a risk of any consequence for looks' sake."

Early on the morning of February 23, the train carrying Abraham Lincoln on the final leg of his long journey pulled into Washington, D.C. This time, no crowds greeted him. This was a slave-holding city, too, and many of its residents wished him ill—or dead. Nine dangerous days remained before his scheduled inauguration. And many enemies continued to issue threats—warning that he would never live to take the oath of office on March 4.

Mary, Bob, Willie, and Tad followed into Washington later that same day. After a twelve-day railroad journey—and an amazing total of 101 speeches by the exhausted president-elect—the family was safely united in the capital of the divided country he had been chosen to lead.

Over the next week and a half, the Lincolns settled into a fine suite of rooms at Willard's Hotel, the best spot in the city. There they held receptions, entertained

The new, unfinished dome of the U.S. Capitol rises under a nest of scaffolding on Lincoln's inauguration day, March 4, 1861.

famous visitors, and prepared for the move to the White House. They also made a point of seeing the well-known sights, including the Washington Monument, which was then only a half-completed stump rising not from today's Mall but from what was then a filthy swamp. Even the now-famous U.S. Capitol dome was still under construction. Many years had passed since the Lincolns' last visit. But Washington, D.C., remained a muddy, unfinished city. It was not the beautiful capital we know now, but a work in progress.

Yet Washington was still full of wonders like the new Smithsonian Institution. When he wasn't accompanying his father on walks around the city, Bob got to tour the Patent Office building. There, he viewed the little wooden model of a ship that his father had carved many years earlier. Lincoln had once hoped this "invention," based on a scheme for lifting boats above shallow waters, would earn him fame and fortune. It did neither, but at least Lincoln became the only president of the United States ever to hold a patent. Now Robert saw the model ship for himself.

The family rose early on inauguration day, March 4, 1861. Before he joined outgoing president James Buchanan for the parade down Pennsylvania Avenue to the Capitol, Lincoln decided he had one more important task to fulfill: he must rehearse his inaugural address out loud a final time. To help him through this last practice session, Lincoln turned to the young man who had nearly lost the speech just a few days earlier. Using Bob as his sounding board, the president-elect read the entire speech from start to finish—an honor his son never forgot.

No one is absolutely sure how many Lincolns attended that day's ceremonies. Mary was certainly there, sitting in the separate section reserved for ladies. So, of course, was Bob—somewhere in the audience of special guests sitting on the east porch of the United States Capitol to watch the new president take his oath. We do not know for certain whether their parents allowed Willie and Tad to join the vast throng gathered there, but it is certainly possible that they attended with their mother.

As many as twenty thousand people crowded the plaza for the spectacular event—the largest crowd ever to attend a presidential inaugural up to that time. As he took his place on the portico, Lincoln could look out and see a statue of his hero, George Washington. The view would remind him not only of the nation's past, but of his own. For he could also see the site of Mrs. Sprigg's old boarding house, where he and his young family had stayed fourteen years earlier, when he

Though impossible to identify Abraham Lincoln at his first inaugural, he is somewhere on the Capitol porch, under the little wooden canopy built there to shield him from the sun. This is one of the earliest photographs of a presidential inauguration.

The White House as it looked in the early days of the Civil War. The platform encircling the tall pole on the lawn was used by the president for flag-raising ceremonies.

last served in this city as a congressman. There was much for him to be proud of on this unforgettable day. Yet the new president appeared "pale and very nervous."

Before taking his oath, Lincoln unfolded and then delivered the address that his son had almost lost two weeks earlier. It was a firm speech—warning the South that it must remain loyal to the Union. But it ended with a warm plea to "the better angels of our nature" for calm and unity. "We must not be enemies," he declared, but friends. "Though passion may have strained, it must not break our bonds of affection."

But as Lincoln likely knew, those "bonds" were already so frayed they could no longer be repaired. The new Confederate States of America had installed Jefferson Davis as president even before Lincoln could take the oath as president of the United States. North and South could no longer resolve their differences over slavery. The house had divided after all. Would it be "peace," Lincoln now wondered, or "a sword?"

Later on that memorable afternoon of March 4, the Lincolns moved into the White House, the biggest and most famous home in America. But it would not prove a happy home for the Lincoln boys or their parents. And it would not be a happy time for their country.

Mary Lincoln was a well-dressed First Lady. But many Northerners thought her lavish spending on the latest fashions showed poor judgment during wartime.

Robert poses in a Washington photo gallery around July 1861—the month of the Battle of Bull Run, the beginning of the Civil War. He had just graduated from Exeter and passed his Harvard entrance test on his second try.

CHAPTER TEN
Running Wild in the White House

Bob Lincoln spent only a brief time at the new president's new mansion. The very day after the inauguration, as a newspaper reported, he already declared himself "sick of Washington and" eager "to get back to his college." Soon thereafter, he returned to Massachusetts to continue his education at Harvard. Lincoln's eldest son later admitted that, during the entire time his father served as president, he "never unpacked his trunk at the White House."

Bob's separation from his parents was now all but complete. For the next four years, he visited Washington only occasionally and, when he did, rarely spent much time with his parents. In fact, he confessed, he seldom enjoyed any private time at all with his father from that day forward. "I scarcely even had ten minutes quiet talk with him during his Presidency," he admitted "on account of his constant devotion to business."

Few of his homecomings proved entirely happy, either. Like most college students, then as well as now, Bob had his own ways and did not like the idea of returning to his parents' home to be told what to do. Whenever he headed back to Washington, he preferred spending his time with his father's young secretary John Hay or with friends his own age—female as well as male. He had little patience for his wild little brothers. And besides, Bob had now convinced himself that he was more refined, elegant, and well schooled than his parents. Like many teenagers of his time and ours, he often found himself embarrassed by his father and mother— no matter how famous they had become. But back at Harvard, Robert promptly suffered a rude reminder that he was still a child himself: he caught the mumps. At least he was far from Washington when his younger brothers came down with yet another childhood disease—measles.

Once recovered, Lincoln's younger boys came to regard their first year in the White House as the greatest adventure of their lives—and their greatest challenge, too. The big new home offered Willie and Tad endless opportunities for exploring—and making mischief.

Mary's cousin thought the White House into which the Lincoln family moved in 1861 was "shabby." Indeed, the new First Lady quickly launched a costly project aimed at redecorating the run-down presidential home. For his part, Lincoln thought it was "better than any house *they* had ever lived in."

Shabby or otherwise, here in this vast, historic mansion, complete with servants, doormen, groundskeepers, gardeners, and soon soldiers, too, Willie and Tad could invent all the games and fantasies they had ever dreamed about. And just as he had reacted back in Springfield, Lincoln, of course, found all their schemes delightful.

At first, it did not matter much to the children that North and South soon began fighting a horrific, bloody civil war. The sight of uniformed soldiers and dangerous weapons on the White House grounds only added to their excitement. In the spring of 1861, Confederate troops pushed so close to Washington that some people urged the new president to take his family and flee the city. Lincoln would not hear of it. And Mary, who still resented the fact that she had been forced to let her husband begin his inaugural journey without her, refused to budge, too. Troops finally arrived from Massachusetts to protect the president, his wife, and sons. Shortly thereafter, in mid-April, Confederate guns opened fire on Fort Sumter, a federal garrison in the harbor of Charleston, South Carolina. The war of words between North and South had now become a war of cannons and shells.

Then on May 24, the family suffered a tragic loss almost as haunting as the death of their own beloved Eddy. Their young friend Elmer Ellsworth was now commanding his own unit of Zouave soldiers. That day he decided to march them across the Potomac River into nearby Alexandria, Virginia. For days, one of that town's hotels had been defiantly flying a Confederate flag that could be seen all the way from the White House. Ever loyal to Lincoln, Ellsworth thought it his duty to remove this offense to his president.

Ellsworth reached the hotel, then bravely marched up to its roof and yanked down the Rebel flag. But as he made his way downstairs, clutching the flag in his arms, the furious hotel owner aimed a shotgun at the little colonel and fired his

The Civil War began here—at Fort Sumter in Charleston Harbor, South Carolina. Southern troops opened fire on the federal outpost on April 12, 1861. After nearly two full days of bombardment, its small garrison of U.S. troops surrendered and abandoned Sumter.

weapon, killing him instantly. When news of young Ellsworth's sudden death reached the Lincolns, they were grief-stricken. The brave colonel's body was carried back to the White House for an official funeral. The violence had suddenly come home to the Lincoln family.

The family's grief did not stop Tad from waving Ellsworth's captured Confederate flag one day at a White House ceremony for Union soldiers. The troops looked on in horror as the little scamp displayed the enemy banner. On this occasion, Lincoln's famous patience finally snapped. When he spotted the boy waving the banner, he promptly hoisted him into his arms, handed him off to a White House servant, and ordered him removed from the scene.

That July, only a few weeks after Ellsworth's death, Union and Confederate troops met for the first big fight of the war. It was the Battle of Bull Run in the nearby Virginia town of Manassas. Unexpectedly, the outnumbered Southerners won the battle against the larger Union army. Beaten badly, federal soldiers limped home to Washington in humiliation. It was now clear to all that it would be a long and costly war.

Sleeping but little, deeply agitated about his army's loss to these powerful

Confederate forces, Lincoln greatly enjoyed whatever distractions his boys offered. One of the president's secretaries wrote that Lincoln's younger sons provided immense joy to their burdened father as they "came and went . . . at their own childish will."

One morning, this same secretary arrived at his office next to the president's to find the green cloth of his worktable smeared with ink and cut to shreds. What had happened? "Tad and Willie Lincoln have been here," he quickly realized, "and they are the happy owners of brand-new pocket knives. They are sharp knives, too, that will cut . . . cloth table-covers . . . or of anything else." Lincoln, of course, thought the prank was funny.

On another memorable day, the boys were busily exploring the White House when they discovered a tiny attic room that housed a pile of bundled-up wires. The wires rang the bells that summoned servants to the various downstairs rooms. Soon all the bells were ringing through the mansion at the same time. Willie and Tad had seized the wires and were gleefully tugging them all simultaneously. Their father ordered them down from the attic, but naturally did nothing to punish them.

Willie and Tad became happy partners in crime, yet their very different personalities also set them apart from each other. The older Willie seemed, to John Hay, "a peculiarly promising boy." A visitor noted admiringly that he could sit quietly for hours, reading alongside his mother in the White House library. Dealing with others, he could be as formal as a diplomat. While playing alone one morning on the lawn, he was introduced to some dignified-looking strangers. To be polite, the visitors bowed and greeted him. Willie bowed right back, pointed to the ground, and gravely replied: "Gentlemen—I am very happy to see you—pray be seated."

But plump little Tad remained "full of merry mischief, the ludicrous effect of which was in no way lessened by the impediment in his speech whenever he was called to account"—which was "not very often."

Few people could understand Tad's odd way of speaking—save for his parents. For example, the boy could not say the word *Lib*, the nickname for Lizzie Keckly, his mother's seamstress; he pronounced it *Yib*. Nor could Tad say *Papa dear*, his pet name for his beloved father. He pronounced it *Papa day*. It would be years before Mary attempted to have Tad's damaged palate repaired by doctors. Meanwhile, his father often acted as Tad's "interpreter."

That October, the family suffered yet another terrible loss. Old friend Edward

Baker, their dead son's namesake, was killed at the Battle of Ball's Bluff near Leesburg, Virginia, another embarrassing defeat for the Union. A heartbroken Lincoln attended Baker's funeral. But the ever-sensitive Willie did more. Though he was not quite eleven years old, he wrote his own poem in Baker's honor. He sent it to the *Washington National Republican* newspaper with a note modestly explaining: "I enclose you my first attempt at poetry. Yours truly, William W. Lincoln." His father must have been extremely proud when Willie's impressive tribute appeared in print on November 4, 1861:

> *There was no patriot like Baker,*
> *So noble and so true;*
> *He fell as a soldier on the field,*
> *His face to the sky of blue.*
>
> *His voice is silent in the hall,*
> *Which oft his presence grac'd,*
> *No more he'll hear the loud acclaim,*
> *Which rang from place to place.*
>
> *No squeamish notions filled his breast,*
> *The Union was his theme,*
> *"No surrender and no compromise,"*
> *His day thought and night's dream.*
>
> *His country has her part to play,*
> *To'rds those he has left behind,*
> *His widow and his children all—*
> *She must always keep in mind.*

There was no question that talented and thoughtful William Wallace Lincoln had become the president's favorite child. He was clearly "a remarkably bright boy for one of his years," with an astonishing memory. He needed only to glance at a book once or twice to retain its contents—forever. In such ways, Willie often reminded Lincoln of himself. Watching Willie one day thinking hard about some problem, then suddenly looking up and smiling at the moment he figured out the solution, Lincoln happily announced: "I know every step of the process by which that boy arrived at his satisfactory solution of the question before him." As Lincoln proudly pointed out: "It is by just such slow methods I attain results." Mary remembered Willie as "different from most children in his ways," happy "to sit and gaze, absorbed in thought." When she interrupted him, he would reply: "Oh, mother, I am thinking of a great many things!"

Mary was certain that when he grew up, Willie would become "the hope" of her "old age." She expected little from the rambunctious Tad, whom she called her "merry sunshine." To Mary, despite the war, the family seemed to be enjoying "*much bliss*" during their first months in the White House. "We have only to give our orders for the dinner," she bragged to a friend, "and *dress* in proper season." They could "order" up something else as well: new friends for the boys.

Starting in March 1861, the three children of a Washington judge named Horatio Taft became Willie and Tad's favorite playmates: Julia, Bud, and their brother, Holly. The boys were eight and twelve, very close in age to Willie and Tad. Julia acted as a kind of unofficial baby-sitter. "Willie was the most lovable boy I ever knew," Julia recalled, "bright, sensible, sweet-tempered and gentle-mannered." Tad, on the other hand, had what she called "a quick and fiery temper" and was affectionate only "when he chose."

The Lincoln boys became fast friends with the Tafts. They invited them to Easter egg rolling on the White House lawn and frolicked with them inside the mansion's private rooms. Julia remembered that however badly the war was going that first year, their father's rule was "Let the children have a good time."

Willie and Tad soon decided they much preferred the Taft family's church services to the ones their parents attended. As they told their mother, Sunday worship at the Tafts' church seemed "livelier"—and certainly a good deal briefer. Tad asked his father, "why do the preachers always pray so long for you, Pa?"

"Well, Tad," answered the president, "I suppose it's because the preachers think I need it and I guess I do."

What Lincoln seemed to need most of all was relaxation time with his children. Whenever the exhausted president entered the White House sitting room, the boys and the Taft children pounced on him, wrestled with him, or demanded that he tell them a story. He particularly enjoyed spinning tales of ferocious Indian attacks, even if the stories ended, as they often did, with the Indians escaping unharmed. "But they got away, Pa, they got away," Tad would protest. "Oh, yes, they got away," Lincoln answered. Then, standing up to leave, he added: "Now *I* must get away."

One day, Julia heard a particularly loud commotion coming from one of the White House rooms and rushed in to find the gigantic president lying on his back, pinned to the floor, with Willie, Tad, Bud, and Holly all struggling to hold him down. When the boys spied the older girl in the doorway, they shouted: "Julie, come quick and sit on his stomach." Too embarrassed to participate, Julia fled the scene.

The Taft girl was equally horrified when Tad somehow got hold of a gun. "You're not fit to have a revolver, Tad Lincoln," she said, "and I ought to tell your mother." Of course, it was Tad's father who had allowed him to have the weapon in the first place. One day, however, Lincoln sent a worried telegram to Mary when she was traveling with the youngster in New York: "Think you had better put 'Tad's' pistol away. I had an ugly dream about him."

Tad went wild for all things military. His father had a little Zouave uniform made to fit his tiny frame. Now he could look like Ellsworth! Tad proudly wore his

Bud (left) and Holly Taft were the Lincoln boys' best friends. Mary banned them from the White House after Willie died in 1862. She could no longer bear to look at them because they reminded her too much of her late son.

Tad loved all things military, and his father cheerfully supplied him with toy guns, a pony, and, as seen here, a miniature uniform he wore for this 1861 photo. He holds his rifle at port arms. The boy impishly inked in a moustache, beard, and belted sword.

new soldier's suit to have his picture taken. He even held a tiny child-size rifle to pose for the camera. When he got the finished picture home, Tad was dissatisfied. So he picked up a pen and used black ink to draw a fake beard and moustache onto his face, as well as a sash to his waist, all to make him look both fiercer and older. Tad loved the idea of photography. He seemed somehow to sense that pictures of his father had become important tools for keeping Northern spirits high. Pictures of Lincoln suffering seemed to endear him more to his admirers. Once, Tad showed one of his cousins another picture of himself "with great pride," but then hoisted a photo of his father and shouted, "Hurrah for Abe Lincoln!"

Both Lincoln boys loved tagging along with the soldiers who were soon encamped on the White House grounds to protect the president or await orders to march south. Thousands more troops could be found stationed around the Capitol or in other campsites around the city that the boys visited with their mother or father. Soon, sadly, the city was filled with military hospitals, too, which the Lincolns often visited to bring comfort to the wounded.

Most of all, the boys enjoyed riding off with their father to review the lines and lines of soldiers who often assembled to greet their commander in chief. It was always a dazzling sight, even if their tall father sometimes looked terribly awkward in the saddle, his pants riding up so the troops could see his long underwear peeking out. Sometimes the men even laughed at him, though they took to lovingly calling him "Father Abraham" as if he were their own parent. Soldiers began enlisting in the army and marching to a new song: "We are coming, Father Abraham, 300,000 more!" Lincoln remained a father to his own boys but, sadly, had less and less time for them. Robert, Willie, and Tad now had to share "Father Abraham" with hundreds of thousands of other boys.

One day, Mary strictly forbade Willie and Tad from joining one of these military reviews. The boys had come down with bad colds and needed to stay indoors. People who witnessed the spectacle that day first saw the president riding down the line and saluting his troops as formally as he could. Following close behind, however, was a not-so-dignified sight: a rickety wooden cart pulled by a mule and steered by an elderly African American. The Lincoln boys had used their own pennies to hire the old man and his wagon, defying their mother to attend the event. Anything to see the army men on parade.

On another occasion, the president joined General Joseph Hooker for a large review of Union cavalry. As Lincoln looked on, squadrons of troops galloped by at great speed. They kicked up so much wet dirt that their uniforms were soon splattered with mud. A few riders fell off their horses onto the slippery ground. But in the midst of all flew Tad, "clinging to the saddle of his pony as tenaciously as the best man among them, his gray cloak flying at the head." Muddy trails were not enough to keep Tad from the soldiers.

Tad soon had a soldier of his very own: a doll named Jack. One day, the boy gravely reported to his father that it had fallen asleep while on guard duty and—like real-life soldiers who had committed the same offense—was scheduled to be shot. Tad insisted that the president do for Jack what he had done for many young men in the same situation: forgive him and spare his life. It was just pretend, but Lincoln played along. Smiling, the president of the United States wrote out a formal command as if the case were real: "The Doll Jack is pardoned by order of the President. A. Lincoln."

It was hard for anyone—playmates, parents, or teachers—to control the young Lincoln boys. Willie and Tad did as they pleased, when they pleased, and where they pleased. One day, Tad was seen wearing one of his father's favorite top hats.

Top left: Seven-year-old Tad poses in his summer suit in July 1861, five months after the Lincoln family arrived in Washington.

Top right: This 1861 picture of Willie was not known to the public during the White House years. But Mary carefully preserved it in her family album. A White House clerk called Willie "a particularly promising boy."

Right: Willie (center) and Tad pose with their mother's cousin Lockwood M. Todd, who visited Washington in 1861 to ask the president for a government job. Several Todd relatives asked for such appointments, even though, like Lockwood, they were Democrats who had not supported Lincoln for president. Most were hired anyway.

Asked why he had taken it, the imaginative child replied that he hoped wearing it would cause his head to sweat and "make my hair grow." Lincoln once asked Willie and Bud to go shopping and buy him some galoshes, suggesting they look for the largest size they could find. Typically, Willie took the responsibility seriously. He sneaked off to his father's bedroom, borrowed one of the giant boots in his closet, and lugged it along to the shoemaker's. The boys did not tell the shopkeeper for whom the rubbers were meant, but the owner thought he must have the largest feet in all of Washington.

Willie and Tad soon welcomed yet another "family" to the White House—a menagerie of pets of all kinds. In addition to kittens, they were given their very own ponies, and Tad became a fine horseback rider—fearless, it was said. The boys somehow got hold of their own team of goats, too, hitching them up to a wagon and noisily riding down the second-floor hallway of the White House as servants and guests alike scattered to get out of the way. Ward Hill Lamon remembered that Lincoln "loved Tad's cats" but loved his goats "less." Still, the president objected when a White House guard complained that one of the goats was too much trouble. "It interests the boys," he replied, "and does them good; let the goat be." Other pets continued to run unleashed through the mansion, too.

The boys also loved to stage their own plays and circuses, sometimes demanding that servants and guards either join them on their "stages" for these performances or pay them for the "privilege" of watching them. White House carpenters eventually installed a little theater for them in one of the spare rooms—where they could perform their own childlike productions and entertain family and staff. Eventually, a local theater owner helped decorate the area with curtains and scenery.

Formal education came last. Instead of attending school, Willie and Tad took lessons in the White House from Alexander Williamson, a private tutor. Willie enjoyed his lessons and, like his father and mother, developed a keen love of reading. As for Tad, White House secretary John Hay put it this way: "He had a very bad opinion of books." The truth is, Tad did not learn to write until he was a teenager.

Both boys "kept the house in an uproar," claimed Hay. "They drove their tutor wild with their good-natured disobedience; they organized a minstrel show in the attic; they made acquaintance with the office-seekers, and became the hot champions of the distressed." They built a pretend boat on the roof, named it the *Ship of State*, and organized war games there.

Yet the boys were unselfish. Their hearts always went out to strangers, even those demanding favors from their father. They developed a high opinion—higher than most—about the many visitors who thronged into the White House nearly every day, especially the mothers of soldiers who had been wounded or killed in action. As these callers lined up outside Lincoln's office to wait their turn, Willie and Tad often came out to talk to them and express sympathy for their hopes and schemes. Sometimes they even urged their patient father to be kinder to the relatives.

The president had been avoiding one such group for days when Tad found them in a hallway and took a liking to them. Within minutes, he was breaking through the long lines of people, pushing his way into his father's office, and insisting that he see them immediately. Later, his father asked him: "Tad, why did you do that?" Answered the boy: "I thought they were your friends, and they looked so sorry." "That's right, my son," his father gently told him. "I would have the whole human race your friends and mine, if that were possible."

Whatever the president was doing—whomever he was meeting—he always tried to find time for the boys. White House secretary William Stoddard saw "both or either come and stand by their father's knee," even "when grave statesmen and pompous generals were presenting to him matters of national or world-wide importance." The boys' interruptions, Stoddard came to realize, "were of more value to their father and to his work than anyone knew."

Losing one of those boys proved the darkest event of the Lincolns' life—and for Tad, too, the saddest moment he had ever known.

Soldiers crowded Washington during the Civil War—using the city as a campsite, training ground, and hospital. Willie and Tad loved seeing the men in uniform and made friends with many of the troops who made camp around the White House.

President Lincoln and the First Lady never posed together before the cameras. But clever photographers pasted together separate pictures of them. They issued fakes like this one and called them genuine. Had Mary really stood next to her husband for a photo, she would of course have appeared much shorter than she seems here.

Abraham Lincoln seemed to age quickly once he became president. This photo was taken in 1862.

CHAPTER ELEVEN
Losing "the Idolized One"

The Lincoln family's second year in the White House began with great hope. It did not last.

In early January of 1862, Mary made sure Bob got free railroad passes from Boston to Washington so he could return for winter vacation at the White House. Now the entire family would be together again for a reunion.

Then on February 6, a week before the president's fifty-third birthday, a new Union general named Ulysses S. Grant captured Fort Henry from the Confederates in Tennessee. Just two days later, the Union won a small but important victory on Roanoke Island in North Carolina. And on the thirteenth, Grant struck again, this time at Fort Donelson on the Cumberland River in Tennessee. The Confederate stronghold surrendered to Union forces two days later. It suddenly seemed as if Lincoln and his armies might finally be blessed with good fortune.

But the luck did not hold at home. Sometime in late January or early February, the beloved Willie took ill. He probably became sick from the drinking water in Washington. The White House bathrooms and kitchens were very modern by the standards of the day. After all, the Lincolns' home back in Springfield boasted no indoor plumbing like the president's mansion did. But the White House drew its "up-to-date" water supply from the nearby Potomac, a swampy river polluted by the decaying bodies of dead animals. John Hay thought it stank of "the ghosts of 20,000 dead cats." Making matters even worse, the soldiers who camped near the river used it as a toilet.

No one can explain why Willie alone became so gravely sick that cold winter. (Though Tad suffered a bout of serious illness, too, he would eventually recover.)

It was Willie who caught the most severe case of typhoid fever, a disease from which few Americans suffer today. In 1862, however, doctors were helpless to treat it.

At the time Willie fell ill, Mary Lincoln was in the midst of preparing for her first big White House party—a highly important occasion for her. Guests were to attend by invitation only, an unheard-of formality for the Executive Mansion until then. The entire capital seemed gripped with excitement over the ball. Washington desperately needed a glittering event to reawaken its spirits. When Willie's fever spiked, however, a concerned Mary wanted to cancel the party. But after consulting a leading doctor, who insisted the boy was in no real danger, her husband advised her to continue as if nothing were wrong, because the ball was so important both to Mary and to the unhappy city.

Unfortunately, by the time the reception got underway on the evening of February 5, Willie had grown much worse. He remained confined to bed, sweating and vomiting, suffering intense pain as his intestines began to bleed. Abraham and Mary reluctantly dressed and went downstairs to greet their guests. But all through the night, the worried parents took turns rushing back up to visit Willie, hold his hand, and anxiously ask doctors if he was getting any better. He was not.

Willie grew steadily weaker. He slept much of the time—occasionally calling out for his friend Bud Taft, who stayed close to his bedside. Lincoln wandered into the sickroom every so often to lovingly run his huge hands through his suffering son's hair. At one point, Lincoln urged Bud to get some rest of his own, but Willie's loyal pal would not give up his vigil. "If I go he will call for me," he explained.

Just after sundown on February 20, 1862, as his parents looked on helplessly, William Wallace Lincoln died. He was only eleven years old. Lincoln staggered out of his favorite boy's bedroom and walked down the long hallway to the office where his secretary sat. There, with eyes red and face worn and pale, he announced the tragic news: "Well, Nicolay, my boy is gone—he is actually gone." Then, as his entire body shook with grief, he burst into loud sobs and limped out of the room.

As tragedy seized the White House, the rest of Washington continued to "rejoice" at the army's recent victories. But a night of official celebration, on which every building in the city was to be brightly lit, was postponed out of

Mary Lincoln in 1863, still dressed in black (and wearing black mourning jewelry) in memory of Willie, more than a year after his death. Mary described herself at the time as in "the *deep waters*" of despair.

respect for the Lincolns' recent loss. Thousands gathered to celebrate the victories at the Capitol building and hear a guest speaker read George Washington's famous farewell address. But the president, because of what was described as his "family affliction," did not attend.

A few hours later, as Willie's body was being prepared for burial, Lincoln returned for one more look at his lost child. As seamstress Lizzie Keckly watched silently, the president "buried his face in his hands, and his tall frame was convulsed with emotion." Lizzie could not believe that "his rugged nature could be so moved."

"My poor boy," he cried aloud, "he was too good for this earth. God has called him home. I know that he is much better off in heaven, but then we loved him so. It is hard, hard to have him die." An old friend understood Lincoln's immense sorrow: "He was fonder of that boy than he was of anything else."

Lincoln had glimpsed so many of his own traits in his son: a wonderful sense of humor coupled with growing wisdom, talent for writing, and sympathy with others less fortunate. "Dear Willie," playmate Julia Taft agreed. "He was pure gold." But most crushing of all was that of all the president's sons, it was Willie who seemed to have the brightest future. With "all of his boyish frolic," White House secretary John Hay agreed, Willie was "a child of great promise, capable of close application and study." And now he would realize none of it.

Despite Lincoln's anguish, no one ever claimed that the president's profound mourning ever took much time away from his official duties. John Hay marveled that throughout his ordeal the president "kept about his work the same as ever." Remarkably, he "gave no outward sign of his trouble."

For weeks, though, Lincoln spent each Thursday, the same day Willie had died, locked away for hours in his room, refusing to see anyone. A minister was summoned to counsel him and told the grieving father: "Your son is alive in Paradise." "Alive! Alive!" came the president's anguished reply. "Surely you mock me." But after he considered the minister's words, his pain finally eased.

Lincoln found additional comfort from books—particularly Shakespeare. Especially helpful was Shakespeare's tragedy *King John*. Over and over, the president read its achingly sad speech in which the character Constance bemoans the loss of a son of her own.

One day, Lincoln read it aloud to a colonel named Le Grand Cannon. His voice was trembling as he recited this passage:

Grief fills the room up of my absent child,
Lies in his bed, walks up and down with me,
Puts on his pretty looks, repeats his words,
Remembers me of all his gracious parts,
Stuffs out his vacant garments with his form;
Then have I reason to be fond of grief.
Fare you well: had you such a loss as I,
I could give better comfort than you do . . .
O Lord! my boy, my Arthur, my fair son!
My life, my joy, my food, my all the world!

After finishing the reading, Lincoln solemnly turned to Colonel Cannon and wondered aloud: "Did you ever dream of some lost friend and feel that you were having a sweet communion with him, and yet have a consciousness that it was not a reality?" Then Abraham Lincoln admitted: "That is the way I dream of my lost boy Willie." Overcome with emotion, the tired leader let his head fall into his arms and began sobbing aloud.

Eventually, Lincoln began taking comfort from these dreams. In a way, they brought Willie back. One day, the president asked Secretary of the Treasury Salmon Chase, "Do you ever find yourself talking with the dead?" Then he confided: "Ever since Willie's death, I catch myself involuntarily talking to him, as if he were with me, and I feel he is." It became his sole comfort.

The other Lincolns had even more difficulty grieving. When Tad heard the news of his beloved brother's death, he actually fell to the floor in grief. But Mary took Willie's death hardest of all. When she first saw Willie's body, she broke into loud and violent convulsions. Just as when Eddy died, she became—and remained—hysterical. The grief-stricken mother was taken to bed and remained there for weeks. She was unable to do anything to help Tad, who soon fell sick as well. Together with Abraham and Bob, she managed to pay one last private visit to the Green Room of the White House, where Willie's coffin now rested. But she collapsed yet again and was led back to bed. Mary could not bring herself to attend Willie's White House funeral, much less accompany his little coffin to a nearby Georgetown cemetery, where he was temporarily laid to rest in a burial vault. Lincoln made the sad journey without her.

With rare exceptions, Mary could neither see friends nor answer letters of sympathy. "We have met with so overwhelming an affliction in the death of our beloved Willie[,] a being too precious for earth," she explained to one of her former neighbors in Springfield, ". . . I can scarcely command myself to write." As she put it to one of her few Washington friends, "how the heart bleeds" over "our precious lambs." She soon came to refer to her "crushing bereavement" for her "sainted boy" as her "fiery furnace of affliction."

Mary now put all the fancy clothes for which she was famous—and so often criticized—into storage. To replace them she ordered plain black dresses and veils—buying many more than she could ever possibly use. She ordered Willie's bedroom locked up and never entered it again. She even canceled the free weekly White House band concerts that the public loved so much—not just for weeks, but for months—until the president himself finally had to overrule her and allow them to resume.

As for Willie's loyal playmates, Bud and Holly Taft, Mary banned them from the funeral, then refused to allow them back inside the White House, even though Tad now needed friends more than ever. She explained that she simply could not bear to look at the happy Taft children again because they would only remind her of Willie. "It makes me worse to see them," she insisted. The Taft boys never even got to say good-bye to Tad.

Mary's outbursts of violent sobbing continued for weeks with no end in sight. Then one day an exasperated Lincoln suddenly took her by the arm to a White House window and pointed to the insane asylum in the distance. "Mother," he said, "do you see that large white building on the hill yonder? Try and control your grief or it will drive you mad, and we may have to send you there."

Then Tad's health worsened, and soon he was fighting for his own life. The little boy was described as "tossing with typhoid" even as he continued to shed tears for the brother he would never see again. Whenever he was able, the president took his paperwork to his youngest boy's bedroom, keeping a watchful eye on him for fear he might lose him, too. Mary often crept into the bedroom, too, tenderly helping her husband off with his tie or removing his boots and replacing them with his slippers. One day, the president told a nurse who was helping care for the boy, "I hope you will pray" for Tad, "and, if it is God's will, that he may be spared—and also for me; for I need the prayers of many." Then he burst into tears and cried out, "This is the hardest trial of my life. Why is it? Oh, why is it?"

Mary thought she knew exactly why. Again she turned to religion—and this time, to beliefs of a different kind—to help her through her unbearable loss. For one thing, Mary convinced herself that God had taken Willie away because she had come to take too much pride in her life as First Lady. In a way, she blamed herself.

"I had become so wrapped up in the world, so devoted to our own political advancement that I thought of little else besides. Our Heavenly Father sees fit, oftentimes to visit us, at such times for our worldliness." Hard as it is to believe, some Americans actually agreed with her. Harsh critics claimed that the Lincolns deserved to lose their child for being too lavish in wartime. God had "interfered," one cruel Washington storekeeper commented, "to put a stop to any more parties at the White House this winter."

For Mary, parties were a thing of the past. She told friends that the glories of living in the White House had lost all meaning for her. Their home was still "very beautiful," she admitted, "the grounds around us are enchanting, the world still smiles & pays homage yet the charm is dispelled—everything appears a mockery." That was because "the idolized one, is not with us, he has fulfilled his mission and we are left desolate."

As Mary lamented: "When I think over his short but happy childhood, how much comfort, he always was to me, and how fearfully, I always found my hopes concentrating on so good a boy as he was—when I can bring myself to realize that [he] has indeed passed away, my question to myself is, 'can life be endured?'"

For a time, she turned to faith in heaven. "God, can *alone*, lighten the burden, until I am reunited to my dearly beloved . . . children," she wrote. But she soon found that this time, God alone was *not* enough to heal her wounded spirit.

So she embraced another kind of belief to help her past her crisis: the very popular but controversial fad at the time known as spiritualism. Convinced that Willie's ghost still hovered "very near" and that only "a very slight veil" separated

The grieving Mary invited spiritualists to the White House in a desperate attempt to contact her dead son in the beyond. To comfort her, the president attended at least one such séance, and this cartoon made the event seem ridiculous.

her from "the 'loved & lost,'" Mary began hosting séances in the White House. She sincerely believed they would enable her to communicate with her dead sons. At these sessions, held in darkened rooms, professional spiritualists who called themselves "mediums" pretended to go into trances and contact the dead. The "spirits" supposedly "answered" with loud raps on tables. These mediums were obvious fakes, but Mary desperately wanted to believe that the séances gave her the ability to keep Willie near her. She held several such sessions at the White House and once even persuaded Lincoln to join her.

Eventually, Mary found some comfort much in the way her husband did: by imagining that she could still see her dead son. "He comes to me every night," she whispered to her cousin, "and stands at the foot of my bed, with the same sweet, adorable smile he has always had; he does not always come alone; little Eddie is sometimes with him." As she told her half sister, Emilie Todd Helm: "If Willie did not come to comfort me, I would still be drowned in tears . . . he lives, Emilie!"

To his mother's and father's great relief, Tad eventually recovered his health and somehow resumed his playful ways. "Dear little Taddie who was so devoted to his darling Brother," Mary wrote, "bears up and teaches us a lesson, in enduring the stroke, to which we *must submit*." In one way, the boy grieved more like his mother than his father. Tad packed up all of Willie's old toys, including two train cars he had loved most of all, and sent them to a cousin in Springfield. He did not want them around to remind him of his lost brother. Like Mary, Tad remained emotionally fragile about Willie. When, two long years later, a now grown-up Julia Taft returned to the White House to attend an afternoon ladies' tea, the boy reacted with horror.

Mrs. Lincoln was courteous to the girl, "but when Tad came in and saw me," Julia sadly recalled, "he threw himself down in the midst of the ladies and kicked and screamed and had to be taken out by the servants."

"You must excuse him, Julia," Mary tried explaining. "You know what he remembers."

The Lincoln Family in the White House

The Lincolns and their boys never posed together as a family, but after the president's death, many artists and photographers invented such scenes to comfort the American public. In truth, the family rarely enjoyed time together during the war years. Though the Lincoln family pictures varied wildly in skill and accuracy (some showed Willie as Tad, or Tad as a drummer boy with long hair), they all appealed to audiences longing to believe that the Lincolns had been happy during the Civil War.

The Lincoln boys' aunt—Mary's sister Elizabeth Todd Edwards—
remained close to the First Lady, even though they often squabbled.
It often seemed as if the Todd sisters were conducting a civil war of
their own.

CHAPTER TWELVE
Lincoln's Little Sunshine

However long and hard he grieved for his dead brother and beloved playmate, Tad Lincoln eventually resumed his routine of fun and adventure in the White House. More than ever, he became his parents' coddled pet and his teachers' worst nightmare. Lonely or not, Tad remained ever mischievous—perhaps more so than before, without the more serious Willie to caution him about his behavior.

Grateful just to have him healthy again, Mary ignored his wildness; he was her "little troublesome *sunshine*." She took him along on her carriage rides, led him off to the country to pick flowers for the injured soldiers at the nearby hospitals, and often asked others to entertain him, too. Once, she begged Colonel Thomas Sweeney of the Internal Revenue Service, whom Tad greatly admired, to join the boy for a horseback ride out to the Washington Navy Yard. "It is, *sometimes*, unfortunate," she flattered the unlucky colonel, "to be a favorite, with so exacting a young *man*."

Though his weary father found it harder and harder to find time to entertain the boy, Tad demanded more and more attention. Every so often, he misbehaved in spectacular ways. One day, for example, his aunt Elizabeth Edwards took the president for a stroll in Lafayette Park across the street from the White House. She had been astonished when Mr. Lincoln told her, "I don't care for flowers—have no natural or Educated taste for Such things." Elizabeth thought that seeing the beautiful park would do the exhausted president much good. Of course, Tad went along, but when his father sadly admitted that he had not visited the park for a year, the little boy concluded that his father must spend more time there than he planned. So he locked the gate and hid the key. Elizabeth and Lincoln became the boy's prisoners. "Mr L. told Tad to get the key. Tad laughed," and of course his father "thought it Smart & Shrewd."

Democrats who opposed the war had been given an insulting nickname: "Copperheads," like the poisonous snakes. When Tad learned of this, he decided to apply shiny black polish to alter a pair of his shoes—which had copper toes. After all, Tad did not want to look like an anti-Lincoln Democrat! An exasperated Mary threatened to punish his vandalism with a whipping. So Tad ran off to his father to beg for mercy, and predictably, Lincoln took his son's side. "I guess I must exercise my executive clemency a little and pardon you, my patriotic boy," Lincoln declared. "You shall not be whipped for this offense." When this story was published a few years later, Mary not only denied "that in my life I have ever whipped a child." But she strained the truth further by adding that her children "never required it, a gentle, loving word" being all they ever needed.

Certainly this was true where their father was concerned. Even when Tad ran completely wild in the White House, Lincoln reacted with sympathy and understanding. "Let him run," he insisted. "There's time enough yet for him to learn his letters and get pokey. Bob was just such a little rascal, and now he is a very decent boy." Excusing Tad totally from school or private tutoring after Willie died, his parents never required that Tad learn much of anything.

The boy "thought very little," John Hay laughed, "of any tutor who would not assist him in yoking his kids to a chair or in driving his dogs tandem over the South Lawn." But even the tutors who threw up their hands in surrender, unable to convince him to master his books, marveled at the way he mastered his pets. Tad had that remarkable "power of taming and attaching animals to himself," a visitor noticed, a truly "special gift." White House guard William H. Crook agreed. "Most boys, by nature," he declared, were "cruel—to each other, to brothers or sisters, to dogs or cats, as we all know. Tad Lincoln never was cruel to any living creature."

In fact, when he grew attached to a large turkey sent to the White House as a gift for the family's Thanksgiving dinner, Tad begged his father to spare the bird's life. "He's a good turkey and I don't want him killed," insisted the boy. Lincoln wrote out an order pardoning the turkey. In return, his grateful son named the bird "Jack" and set him loose in the White House, squawking and flapping his wings.

Lincoln's secretary concluded that the boy he called the "infant goblin" and the "tricksy little sprite" gave "that sad and solemn White House . . . the only comic relief it knew" during the war. Tad's "plots and commotions" kept the White House in constant turmoil until he became "the absolute tyrant of the Executive Mansion." As Hay put it: "He was so full of life and vigor—so bubbling over with health and high spirits, that he kept the house alive with his pranks and his fantastic enterprises."

To Hay, Tad "was a merry, warm-blooded, kindly little boy, perfectly lawless, and full of wild fancies and inventions. . . . He ran continually in and out of his father's cabinet [meetings], interrupting the gravest labors and conversations with his bright, rapid, and very imperfect speech"—for almost no one could understand Tad, it seemed, but his parents. The president, Hay observed, "took infinite comfort" in Tad's "fresh fun, and uncontrollable boisterousness." He seemed not to mind even if Tad "would perch upon his father's knee, and sometimes even on his shoulder, while the most weighty conferences were going on."

On one such occasion, the president was busy in an especially crucial meeting. Suddenly he and his guests were startled by a series of loud bangs on his closed office door: three knocks, followed by two; then three again, followed yet again by two. "Now I wonder what Tadpole wants," Lincoln told his surprised cabinet officers. "You see, that's the code I taught him yesterday, three short and two long. . . . I've got to let him in, you see, because I promised never to go back on the code." Visitors got so used to seeing the boy at the most private meetings that they began keeping vital information to themselves, worried that Tad would hear too much. Even if Lincoln was alone, not all reports were shared with him. As one suspicious guest worried: "He can't keep a secret. He would tell Tad."

Tad's frantic activities would commence early each morning and continue without pause until, exhausted, the boy simply dropped off to sleep on the president's office floor. After finishing his work there hours later, Lincoln "would pick him up and carry him tenderly to bed." The president slept alone down the hall in a huge wooden bed that had a smaller one beneath it—called a trundle bed. Sometimes, Lincoln would pull out the trundle bed and place the sleeping Tad there before he turned off his light. There, Tad would often remain until morning.

Much as he depended on his father, Tad liked to think he alone was in charge of the entire White House. In a way he was. It was his playground, his theater, his army camp, his kingdom, and sometimes his shop. Once, he saw a poor old woman selling gingerbread a few blocks away. On an impulse, he bought all her cakes, took them home, and set up a food stand on a wooden board in front of the majestic White House driveway. By the end of the day, he had sold all the sweets to his father's visitors and made a nice profit. He was quite a sight there, someone recalled, "a rather grotesque-looking little fellow, in his gray trap-door pants . . . and very baggy they were." By nightfall, he had spent every penny. All his new earnings were gone.

Tad dearly loved money and often bribed his willing father: a large coin was demanded in return for good behavior, which at most lasted only briefly. It might take a few cents to get Tad to sit for a lesson or to leave the president's busy office and return to his mother, when he preferred to stay with his father and "see the people." Once, the boy bet both the president and Secretary of State Seward a quarter that they could never guess what kind of animal he had just snared for his growing collection of pets. A rabbit, came the answer. No, that was not it at all, Tad replied, grabbing his twenty-five cents and racing off. Later Lincoln and Seward learned that Tad had indeed become the proud owner of a new rabbit. Neither man asked the scamp for their money back.

In fact, Lincoln became more generous with Tad than ever. He did not care if he spoiled him. Many times he would take his boy to Joseph Stuntz's candy and toy store four blocks from the White House. There he indulged Tad with chocolate caramels, taffy on a stick, or paper umbrellas and tin whistles, all for a penny. Or he might buy the boy one of the more expensive wooden dolls that Mr. Stuntz carved by hand. As Lincoln explained: "I want to give Tad all the toys I didn't have, and all the toys I would have given to the boy who went away."

But much as his father indulged Tad, his behavior did not much improve. In the spring of 1864, a photographer visited the White House to take the president's picture there. It would be the first time any president had ever posed for his photograph inside the mansion. In those days, picture taking was a complicated process, one that only professionals knew how to manage. Photos had to be developed quickly and on the spot. Lincoln assigned the cameraman a small closet on the second floor to set up the necessary chemicals and to use as a darkroom to make his prints. But when the time came to take his newly exposed glass plates there to develop them, the photographer discovered to his dismay that the closet had been locked.

It seemed that Tad claimed the closet as his own private property and was furious that anyone had been allowed to use it without his permission. As the poor cameraman was explaining his dilemma to the president, Tad burst into the office and complained bitterly about the visitor, insisting he "had no business" in his room. Just as he had done at Lafayette Park, he refused to return the key even for the photographer to merely reclaim his smelly chemicals. Lincoln "very mildly" ordered: "Tad, go and unlock the door."

But still Tad refused. Instead he marched into his mother's room, where he planted himself in a chair and stubbornly folded his arms in defiance. Nothing could be done to coax him. Running out of patience, the photographer returned to beg the president to intervene. Lincoln looked up and inquired with mild surprise: "Has not the boy opened that door?"

Pursing his lips—a sure sign to those who knew him that he had made up his mind about something—the president then rose from his own chair and disappeared into the family quarters, looking as if he were "bent on punishment." A few minutes later, he returned with the key and unlocked the closet himself.

"There," he told the cameraman, "go ahead, it is all right now." But, of course, he had not punished the boy at all. As he explained: "Tad is a peculiar child. He was violently excited when I went to him. I said, 'Tad, do you know you are making your father a great deal of trouble?' He burst into tears, instantly giving me up the key."

That same year, Lincoln took Tad to Mathew Brady's famous photography gallery on Pennsylvania Avenue, where he might perhaps learn more about how pictures were made. There they posed together for a now-famous image of father and son looking at a large book. Though the book was in reality only a photo album, it seemed to illustrate the father's loving attention to his son—which often included long hours spent reading aloud to the boy, who had not yet learned to read himself. The picture sold many copies and became quite famous.

"The President never seemed grander in my sight," remembered a visitor from Philadelphia, "than when, stealing upon him in the evening, I would find him with a book open before him as he is represented in the popular photograph, with little Tad beside him. There were of course a great many curious books sent to him, and it seemed to be one of the special delights of his life to open those books at such an hour, that his boy could stand beside him, and they could talk as he turned over the pages, the father thus giving to the son a portion of that care and attention" that his job made so difficult for him to spare.

Abraham and Tad Lincoln posed for this famous picture in Washington on February 9, 1864—three days before the president's fifty-fifth birthday. Father and son are shown looking at a large photo album. It has often been mistaken for a family Bible.

Meantime, Bob took to his books, too—alone up at Cambridge—as he continued his studies at Harvard. Mary visited him there, and the two went off with Tad on vacation to the Vermont mountains. In the hilltop village of Manchester, they found a beautiful hotel called the Equinox, where Mary hoped someday to bring her exhausted husband as well.

The "Prince of Rails" did not always behave like a prince at school. In fact, he occasionally showed the same kind of independent streak he found so disagreeable in his baby brother. In January 1862, early in Bob's college career, Harvard officials warned Lincoln that Bob had become friendly with "some of the idlest persons in his class." His grades were sliding, and he was failing chemistry. Eleven months later, the president of Harvard again found it necessary to write to the president of the United States to report that, this time, Bob had been "admonished for smoking in Harvard Square." The school's leader hoped the nation's leader would "impress upon him" the need for better "decorum."

Lincoln must have been greatly annoyed. He surely believed his oldest son should know better than to dishonor himself at college—especially during a time when so many critics were watching every move the family made. No doubt he wrote him a stern letter or two demanding that he buckle down and change his bad habits. But if he sent such warnings, they have not survived. Bob later made sure he destroyed most of the letters he received from his parents. And this humiliating correspondence may have been the first to go. Yet the warning must have worked. Bob's grades improved. He also joined the school's famous Hasty Pudding Club and pledged for a fraternity.

Like many of his classmates, however, Bob became desperate to leave Harvard and join the army. The war seemed like the great adventure of the age, and Bob wanted to be part of it. His father was sympathetic. After all, Lincoln's political enemies were criticizing him at the time because Bob was *not* in uniform like so many young men his age. Why, they argued, should the president's son escape danger if so many other men's sons were joining up? The anger grew even harsher after Lincoln ordered the country's first military draft. The new law forced young men into uniform whether they wanted to enlist or not. But Mary would simply not hear of the idea of Robert joining the army. Petrified that he would be harmed in

Robert T. Lincoln was a Harvard student when he posed for this photograph in 1862, probably during one of his school breaks in Washington.

battle or, worse, that she might have to bury another son, his mother insisted that Bob remain safely in school. Worried about his wife's emotional health, Lincoln for a time heeded her wishes.

"Son, what are you going to do now?" Lincoln bluntly asked him in 1864. Bob proposed going to law school if he could not enlist. "If you do," came the good-natured answer, "you should learn more than I ever did, but you will never have so good a time." As Bob later put it, with some bitterness: "That is the only advice I had from my father as to my career." In the end, Bob had the best of both worlds. He graduated Harvard and indeed entered Harvard Law School but eventually joined the army as well, over his mother's objections.

Lincoln rarely spoke of his late son Willie—it was too painful for him—but the memory of his loss returned hauntingly one night when the White House stables caught fire. Some whispered that a coachman, angry at being dismissed from his job by Mrs. Lincoln, set the blaze on purpose. The boys' beloved ponies were killed in the raging fire. Lincoln himself tried bravely to save the horses, but guards prevented him from rushing inside the burning building. "Tad was in bitter tears at the loss of his ponies," a member of the White House staff observed. But "his heaviest grief was his recollection that one of them had belonged to Willie."

Another coachman, who lived above the stables, lost around three hundred dollars in cash in that same fire. Bob, who was home from law school at the time, approached his father to ask whether the government shouldn't be responsible for repaying the unlucky fire victim. Lincoln thought it over and replied with a cold legal judgment. Just because the government printed money, it was not obliged to guarantee its value if it was later destroyed. Lincoln instructed his law-student son as if Lincoln were one of his teachers, not just his father; it was "a dead loss" for the coachman. Of course, Bob thought that if Tad had come to his father with the same story, Lincoln would have repaid the coachman out of his own pocket.

As Bob well knew, Lincoln was never so precise when it came to applying the law to his younger brother. Once, Tad took himself to the War Department and asked Secretary of War Edwin Stanton to make him a Union officer. Just for "the fun of the thing," Bob complained, Stanton commissioned Tad a lieutenant colonel. Tad promptly returned to the White House, ordered a stack of rifles, dismissed the official guards, and then demanded that the servants and gardeners assemble to replace them. The staff was long used to obeying the unpredictable little tyrant, so they did as they were told. Tad gave them the guns, and then the brash little "lieutenant colonel" ordered his new "soldiers" to guard his father.

"I found it out an hour ago," Bob testily reported, "and thinking it a great shame, as the men had been hard at work all day, I went to father with it." But "instead of punishing Tad, as I think he ought, he evidently looks upon it as a good joke, and won't do anything about it." Only after Tad had fallen asleep for the

The Lincolns enjoyed going to the theater, and occasionally invited actors and singers to perform in the White House. This drawing shows Lincoln and Tad listening to the Hutchinson Family, famous for their religious songs and hymns.

night did Lincoln quietly dismiss the tired workers and order that the guns be collected and returned to the army. The grateful employees went home, but throughout that night, as a result of Tad's "good joke," the White House had no guards at all!

No act of mischief ever seemed to dismay Tad's father, no matter how naughty. Joining Lincoln once for a boat ride to Fortress Monroe in Hampton Roads, Virginia, Tad began kicking up a fuss while the president was trying to conduct an important conversation. Finally, Lincoln said, "Tad, if you will be a good boy, and not disturb me any more till we get to Fortress Monroe, I will give you a dollar."

Hoping for the reward, Tad quieted down—but only for a while. Soon, a witness observed, he became "as noisy as ever."

But when the boat reached the fort, Tad immediately demanded, "Father, I want my dollar."

Lincoln looked down at him quizzically and inquired, "Tad, do you think you have earned it?"

"Yes," came the defiant reply.

Lincoln took a dollar note from his wallet and handed it to him, sighing, "Well, my son, I will keep *my* part of the bargain."

On yet another memorable occasion, the president declared a national fast day so the nation might give thanks for a recent Union battlefield victory. When Tad heard about the plan, he began stealing treats from the White House kitchen and storing them in a secret place so he could have plenty of food while the rest of the country was doing without. When his father found out about it, he did not scold him. In fact, he seemed rather proud.

"If Tad lives to be a man," predicted the president, "he will be what all women love—a good provider!

The Lincoln family spent three happy summers at this cottage
on the grounds of the Soldiers' Home north of Washington, D.C.
The weather was cooler there, and the president got to relax.
Tad enjoyed riding his pony and visiting the soldiers who
camped on the grounds surrounding the house.

CHAPTER THIRTEEN
Fighting for Freedom

Beginning in the summer of 1862, the Lincoln family dramatically changed its routine. They began spending their summers (and eventually their late springs and autumns, too) at a spacious cottage outside the city. The handsome house stood high on a cool hilltop along the grounds of the Soldiers' Home, a residential community for old and wounded veterans. Here Mary could escape the torrid heat of downtown Washington. Tad could run free and enjoy the company of the men in uniform he adored so much—and who came to adore him as well.

More important, the new vacation house gave the Lincoln family much-needed privacy while still in mourning for Willie. No prying newspaper reporters, and few cranky politicians, traveled to their summer home to lay siege to the president. None were there to criticize his wife for her parties, fancy clothes, or occasional temper tantrums. In this "charming place," as Mary put it, "we can be as secluded, as we please." "When we are in sorrow," she explained, "quiet is very necessary to us."

Whenever the family lived at the Soldiers' Home, Lincoln was forced to ride on horseback or by carriage two and a half miles each way to and from the White House. This he did without complaint, though commuting meant that he had even less time to spend with his wife and child. During one of his late-night rides from downtown Washington, a stranger even took a shot at him. No one ever discovered whether the gun was fired accidentally or on purpose, or by whom. But the bullet came close enough to knock off the presidential top hat. Thereafter, though Lincoln was unharmed, well-armed soldiers always accompanied him on his trips to and from the city.

With his own uniform and miniature weapons, "Lieutenant Colonel" Tad

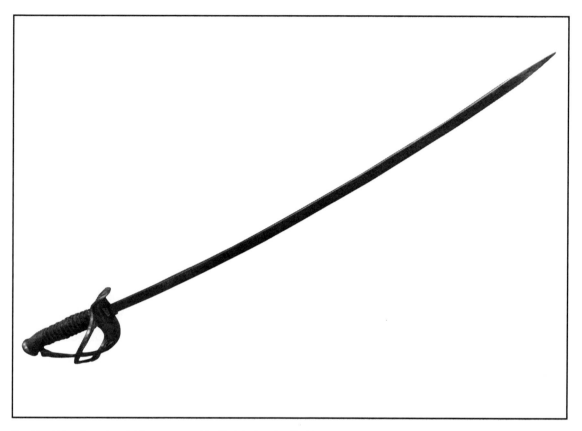

President Lincoln ordered this navy sword for Tad during the Civil War.

Lincoln became "a great favorite" of the military company guarding the Soldiers' Home grounds. They made him an honorary member of their "Bucktail" regiment, complete with a real bucktail to wear on his own little hat. When soldiers assembled to practice their drills, Tad often appeared in full uniform alongside them, astride his lively pony, little legs sticking straight out.

Always famished for some mysterious reason, Tad also enjoyed joining the men at mealtime to share their food. One soldier wrote home to report with amazement that Lincoln's hungry "boy was here yesterday to get something to eat and I gave him Bread and Molasses." Tad often returned home at night with his clothes, hands, and face filthy from campfire soot. But his parents never stopped him from hanging out with the soldiers, because he enjoyed it so.

In the absence of his brother, Tad grew especially close to a skinny, young-looking army private named Philip Yokum. Perhaps he reminded Tad of Willie.

Still, Tad often abused the privileges of being a president's son and ordered Philip about. When the two were detained one day by an army patrol because they lacked a proper pass through the lines, Tad loudly insisted that the commander in chief was his father and he and his friend could go wherever they pleased. After they were released, the boy marched off to see the president and demanded that he write a proper pass that Tad and his friend could use in the future. Lincoln obliged, picking up a piece of official stationery and scribbling: "Guards and Patrols[.] Pass Philip Yocum of the President's Guard. A. Lincoln." Yokum kept the handwritten note for the rest of his life.

Exciting historic events came to pass during the days the Lincolns lived at the Soldiers' Home. In the summer of 1862, the president spent much time there writing the document that would change the war—and change America—forever: the Emancipation Proclamation. The family was still living in their country home when Lincoln announced his decree to the country on September 22. It followed by only a few days the Union victory at the bloody Battle of Antietam in Sharpsburg, Maryland. In his most famous and important order, Lincoln's proclamation warned Rebel states that their slaves would go free "forever" if they did not lay down their arms and rejoin the country by January 1.

As the deadline neared, Mary and Tad journeyed to New York City for a pre-Christmas visit. Mary reported back to the president that "Dear little Taddie is well and enjoying himself very much"—even after the boy lost one of his baby teeth. "I must send you, Taddie's tooth," his proud mother wrote to her husband. But back at the White House, Lincoln's losses were even more painful. He suffered through a terrible Union defeat at the Battle of Fredericksburg. It was one of the worst losses of the entire war.

But the family was reunited by New Year's Day, 1863. That day, despite the embarrassment of Fredericksburg, Lincoln signed the final Emancipation Proclamation. "[W]e cannot escape history," he had told Congress. "In *giving* freedom to the *slave*, we *assure* freedom to the *free*." Slavery—the stain on American democracy that Lincoln had fought against for so many years—was now doomed to die.

Family life changed, too. Bob still came home during school vacations, though at times he seemed even harder to manage than Tad. Aware that his father had but little time for him, Bob preferred spending his breaks in the company of Lincoln's

The words of Lincoln's proclamation were hardly inspiring—they were meant to be legalistic. But artists used them anyway to create tribute portraits—like this one—in calligraphy.

This imaginary scene was published to celebrate the Emancipation Proclamation, issued on January 1, 1863. In truth, Lincoln never personally freed any slaves or broke their chains and shackles, as this print suggests.

secretary John Hay. On one visit to the Soldiers' Home, Bob and John rode together to nearby Fort Stevens, where only a few days earlier a Confederate raiding party not only came dangerously close to the family cottage but also took a few potshots at his father. Bob seemed shocked to see so many "ragged & dirty" Rebel prisoners who told him they wished the war would end so they could return home. He, of course, wanted to leave home and join the war.

As for Tad, peace was the last thing on his mind. It would mean losing his beloved soldiers. He was thrilled, too, when the P. T. Barnum attraction "General Tom Thumb" visited the White House for a February 1863 reception and stayed the night as an honored guest. Tad thoroughly enjoyed meeting the famous three-foot-four-inch "little person" and his equally tiny bride, Lavinia. They were even smaller than he was! The prim and proper Bob did not share his brother's

President and Mrs. Lincoln hosted Tom Thumb and his wife, Lavinia, in February 1863. Robert was embarrassed that such attention was lavished on the famous little couple, but Tad loved meeting adults who were no taller than himself. Mr. and Mrs. "Thumb"—Tom's real name was Charles Stratton—left this photo with the Lincolns as a souvenir.

enthusiasm for circus attractions. Horrified by the undignified event, he huffed to his mother that he had no intention of joining the reception, adding: "my notions of duty, perhaps, are somewhat different from yours."

Bob and his family were growing apart, but Tad was not really growing up. Though ten years old, he still could neither read nor write. And his behavior remained unpredictable. In June 1863, the family was preparing to move to the Soldiers' Home once again when Tad suddenly threw one of his famous temper tantrums and refused to leave. "I have not got my cat," he shouted. He would not permit his parents to budge until it was found. The Great Emancipator himself had no choice but to reenter the White House and search for the missing pet.

Only after a while did the president return holding the lost cat in his arms so the trip finally could commence.

Once settled in for the summer, however, Mary again took Tad off for yet another trip to New York. Lincoln then learned that Robert E. Lee's large Confederate army had marched into Maryland and then up to Pennsylvania. It was Lee's deepest penetration into the North. At first, the president did not seem worried enough to request that his family come home. "I do not think the raid into Pennsylvania amounts to anything at all," he wrote Mary on June 16. He was wrong.

Just two weeks later, on July 1, 1863, hundreds of thousands of Union and Confederate soldiers met at the biggest battle of the entire Civil War: the Battle of Gettysburg. Lincoln's troops defeated the Rebels after three days of intense fighting in the torrid summer heat. The titanic struggle left tens of thousands dead or wounded.

But the joy of a Union victory was clouded by a horrible accident closer to home while the battle still raged. While Mary was out for a ride, the driver's seat on her horse-drawn carriage came loose, throwing the coachman off the vehicle. When the driverless carriage continued to surge wildly along the bumpy road, a terrified Mary panicked and jumped off, falling to the ground and striking her head

The Battle of Gettysburg, July 1–3, 1863, was the largest and bloodiest battle ever fought on the American continent. The Union won, but the president was angry when the army failed to follow General Robert E. Lee's Confederates as they retreated from Pennsylvania to Virginia.

CHARGE OF THE POLICE AT THE TRIBUNE OFFICE.

Just weeks after the Battle of Gettysburg, New York City erupted with a battle of its own—a riot broke out when the first military draft began there. Robert, heading home from college to visit his mother and father, was caught for a time in the city. His absence deeply worried his anxious parents.

on a rock. Some people believed that the driver's seat had been loosened on purpose in a plot to kill the president.

At first Lincoln believed that Mary was only "very slightly hurt," and wrote Bob at Harvard not to be "uneasy." Mary was taken back to the nearby Soldiers' Home to recover in bed. However, Mary's injury became badly infected, and doctors worried that she might die. Lincoln tried to spend time at her side, but with the battle still underway, he was even more agitated and distracted than usual. He secured a nurse to watch over her.

Desperate to get Mary the family attention she needed, Lincoln finally summoned his eldest son back from Cambridge. But more trouble followed. On his way down to Washington, Bob found himself stranded in New York when that city exploded in horrible acts of violence aimed at African Americans. The so-called Draft Riots had begun. Now Lincoln had four things to worry about at once: his wife's critical injury, his son's physical safety, the whereabouts of the Union army, and the rioting in the North's largest city by citizens who opposed being drafted into the army. "Come to Washington," he ordered Bob in a telegram July 11. "Why do I hear no more of you?" he wired anxiously three days later when he learned that mayhem had broken out on the streets of Manhattan.

Bob finally escaped the violence in New York, arrived safely in Washington, and joined the vigil at his mother's bedside. He was home when the president learned to his dismay that Lee's army had not only retreated from Gettysburg but escaped back to Virginia without further challenge from Union forces. Bob found his father "in tears" at the news, "with his head bowed upon his arms." Lincoln told Bob that he believed that Gettysburg had offered the Union a great opportunity for his generals to destroy the Confederate force and end the war. Now he suspected the fighting would continue much longer—with much more death and suffering.

Eventually, Mary's health improved. But Bob always believed that the carriage accident caused her harm from which she never recovered. He insisted that his mother was never quite the same again. Still, Mary did manage to bundle up Tad and take him north for another New England vacation that August. During their absence, Lincoln wrote her with some sad news for his boy: his army of pets had suffered a loss, too. "Tell dear Tad, poor 'Nanny Goat,' is lost," wired Lincoln. "The day you left Nanny was found resting herself, and chewing her little cud, on the middle of Tad's bed [at the Soldiers' Home]. But now she's gone. The gardener kept complaining that she destroyed the flowers, till it was concluded to bring her down to the White House. This was done, and the second day she had disappeared, and has not been heard of since. This is the last we know of poor 'Nanny.'"

Tad received far better news about Fido, the dog he had left behind years earlier in Springfield. Lincoln's old barber, Billy Florville, wrote the president from his old hometown that December: "Tell Taddy that his (and Willys) Dog is alive and Kicking [and] doing well."

This was more than observers could say about Lincoln himself. The lonely president always missed his wife and son when they were off traveling, and longed for them to return. "The air is so clear and cool, and apparently healthy, that I would be glad for you to come," he wrote to Mary when she was in New York on September 21, 1863. "Nothing very particular, but I would be glad [to] see you and Tad."

This time when they returned, it was Tad who took ill. As Mary fretted nervously, the boy came down with a mild case of smallpox. Her husband was scheduled to visit Gettysburg in mid-November to make a short but important speech in tribute to the soldiers who had died at the battle there. But fearful for their boy's health, Mary begged Lincoln not to go. As always, the president's job came first and he left for Pennsylvania as scheduled.

On the morning of November 19, 1863, the president mounted a horse in the Gettysburg town square. He was to lead a solemn procession through town and on to a new cemetery that had just been built to honor the thousands of soldiers who had fallen in battle there in July. Lincoln wore a black ribbon around his high silk hat in memory of those heroes—and of Willie. Just as the parade was set to begin, a messenger arrived and handed him a telegram. No one knows what dark thoughts went through his mind as he tore it open. Was Tad worse? Might he even be dead?

The news turned out to be good. "The Dr has just left," reported Mary. "We hope dear Taddie is slightly better." Greatly relieved, Lincoln moved on to the cemetery. A few hours later, as thousands of people looked on, Tad Lincoln's father gave the most famous speech any American president has ever delivered anywhere.

Though not everyone on the scene

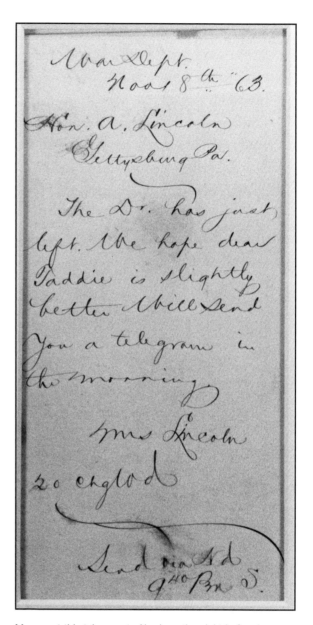

Mary sent this telegram to Abraham the night before he delivered the Gettysburg Address, but according to some accounts, Lincoln opened it the next day. In it she assures her husband that little Tad is recovering from his illness.

appreciated—or even heard—the Gettysburg Address when Lincoln delivered it, its reputation grew as the years went by. Today we regard it as the finest three minutes of Abraham Lincoln's long career as a public speaker. But that evening, as he headed back to Washington by train, Lincoln felt no pleasure—only pain. Suddenly sick himself, he lay down during the train ride home, a wet cloth covering his aching head. Back at the White House, doctors told the president he had caught Tad's smallpox. It was a mild case, not at all life threatening. But it gave Lincoln the longest "vacation" of his presidency to date: two weeks in his sickbed. At one point, even though he was contagious, the president told his

The Gettysburg Address

Four score and seven years ago our fathers brought forth on this continent, a new nation, conceived in Liberty, and dedicated to the proposition that all men are created equal.

Now we are engaged in a great civil war, testing whether that nation, or any nation so conceived and so dedicated, can long endure. We are met on a great battlefield of that war. We have come to dedicate a portion of that field, as a final resting place for those who here gave their lives that that nation might live. It is altogether fitting and proper that we should do this.

But, in a larger sense, we can not dedicate—we can not consecrate—we can not hallow—this ground. The brave men, living and dead, who struggled here, have consecrated it, far above our poor power to add or detract. The world will little note, nor long remember what we say here, but it can never forget what they did here. It is for us the living, rather, to be dedicated here to the unfinished work which they who fought here have thus far so nobly advanced. It is rather for us to be here dedicated to the great task remaining before us—that from these honored dead we take increased devotion to that cause for which they gave the last full measure of devotion—that we here highly resolve that these dead shall not have died in vain—that this nation, under God, shall have a new birth of freedom—and that government of the people, by the people, for the people, shall not perish from the earth.

Abraham Lincoln (bareheaded, circled) sits on the speakers' platform at Gettysburg on November 19, 1863. This photo was taken just hours—perhaps minutes—before he gave the most famous speech in American history.

An artist's view of what Lincoln may have looked like delivering his great Gettysburg Address. No photos were taken while he spoke—for the speech lasted less than three minutes. Lincoln came down with smallpox on his way home from the event, an illness he caught from Tad, who had been sick in bed when the president left for Gettysburg.

secretaries to direct the daily crowd of job seekers to his room. Now, he joked, he had something he could give to everybody.

The new year of 1864 proved to be especially tense for the Lincolns. The war was going badly again, and the public's patience with its president was fading fast.

But Lincoln retained his famous sense of humor. In April, on yet another trip to New York with Tad, Mary wrote to relay the boy's questions about the once-vanished pet goats that he had since either found or replaced: "Tad says are the goats well?"

Replied the president that same day: "Tell Tad the goats and father are very well—especially the goats."

On a warm day that June, Robert graduated from Harvard. Predictably, his father was too busy to travel to Massachusetts to attend the commencement ceremonies. But Mary did go, and watched proudly as Robert T. Lincoln, as he now called himself, just a few weeks shy of his twenty-first birthday, picked up his diploma. A newspaper reported of the recent graduate: "He does everything very well, but avoids doing anything extraordinary."

Robert around 1864—the year he graduated from Harvard College and applied for Harvard Law School. What he really wanted to do was join the Union army, but his worried mother would not permit it.

The president was running for reelection that year, and for most of the summer, it seemed very likely he would lose to the Democrats. Support for the war was wearing thin. Too many men had died, too much money had been spent. Though most Northerners had supported fighting to restore the Union, many of them opposed fighting to free people of color. Still deeply racist, many in the country feared that Lincoln would attempt to make black and white

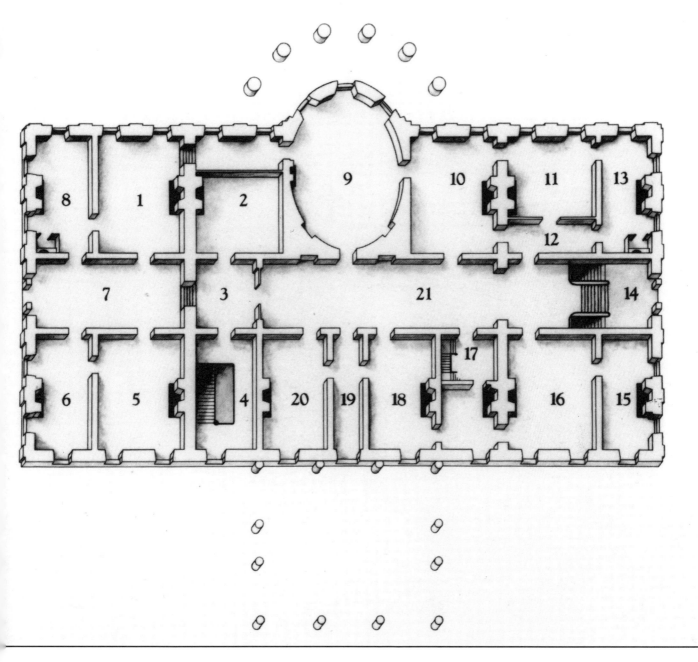

Floor plan of the second-floor offices and family quarters of the White House during Lincoln's time: (1) the president's office; (2) president's reception room, where guests waited; (3) office hallway; (4) stairway down to first floor; (5) bedroom shared by secretaries John Nicolay and John Hay; (6) office shared by clerks Hay and William Stoddard; (7) official waiting room; (8) Nicolay's office with bathroom; (9) family library or "Oval Room"; (10) Mary Lincoln's bedroom; (11) Abraham Lincoln's bedroom; (12) hallway for the master bedroom suite; (13) President and Mrs. Lincoln's dressing room with bathroom; (14) grand staircase; (15) Tad's bedroom; (16) Willie's bedroom, kept locked after he died there in 1862; (17) washroom; (18) guest room; (19) hallway leading to window from which Lincoln occasionally made speeches; (20) guest room; (21) family corridor.

The president's White House office as sketched by C. K. Stellwagen, a visiting artist of the day. At the table in the center, Lincoln held cabinet meetings. On January 1, 1863, he signed the Emancipation Proclamation sitting here. Today, this remodeled chamber is the Lincoln Bedroom.

Americans equal. And this, the majority of whites opposed. Lincoln's chances of victory seemed dim. Only when Union armies captured the city of Atlanta, Georgia, in September did Lincoln's popularity climb back.

On Election Day, November 8, Tad stormed excitedly into his father's office to tell him he had seen soldiers on the White House lawn casting their votes for Lincoln. Tad breathlessly urged his father to the window to watch the scene for himself. A proud Lincoln later learned that 80 percent of all the soldiers in the country had voted to keep him in office for a second term. He won the election with nearly 56 percent of the overall count. Of course, none of the eleven Confederate states participated in the election, or the voting would have been much closer.

But the final result meant that the Lincolns and their boys would remain in the White House. Much as the entire family rejoiced, some still worried.

"Now that we have won the position, I almost wish it were otherwise," Mary confided to her seamstress Lizzie Keckly. "Poor Mr. Lincoln is looking so broken-hearted, so completely worn out, I fear he will not get through the next four years." In fact, he barely survived four *months*. But it was not because of exhaustion.

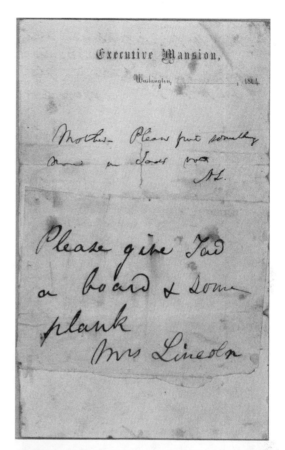

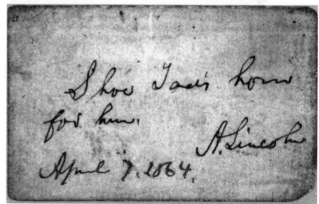

No matter how busy his father was, Tad often burst into the president's White House office seeking attention, affection, and favors. In these two surviving examples of his father's patience and love, the president orders that Tad's bedroom floor be fixed and his horse shod.

This campaign poster for Lincoln's 1864 reelection shows the president alongside his new running mate, Andrew Johnson of Tennessee.

Another campaign picture shows Lincoln as a giant, viewing his Democratic opponent, George B. McClellan, known as "Little Mac," as nothing but a "little joke." Lincoln easily defeated McClellan, winning a second term by a wide margin.

The new Capitol dome was finished by early 1865. Lincoln had refused
to halt construction, though iron was much needed to make weapons.
He believed the finished dome would remind Americans that their
country would survive the Civil War.

CHAPTER FOURTEEN
They Have Killed Papa Dead

Once he graduated college and came of age, there was no stopping Bob from enlisting in the army. There was little even his mother could do to prevent it, even though Mary remained fearful, as she told a longtime Springfield friend, that "the *serpents*" who so often "crossed our pathways" would strike again. As she told her husband: "I know that Robert's plea to go into the Army is manly and noble and I want him to go, but oh! I am so frightened he may never come back to us."

But her husband supported Robert's decision, reminding her: "Many a poor mother, Mary, has had to make this sacrifice and has given up every son she had—and lost them all."

"Don't I know that only too well?" she cried back. Her own half brothers had died fighting—for the Confederacy! "Before this war is ended," she worried, "I may be . . . like my poor mother in Kentucky, with not a prop left in her old age."

In January 1865, Lincoln hit on an idea to please both his wife and his son. He would ask General Ulysses S. Grant, now commanding all Union armies, to give Bob a position on his official staff. Bob, he explained in a letter to the general, "wishes to see something of the war before it ends." But then the president added: "I do not wish to put him in the ranks, nor yet to give him a commission, to which those who have already served long, are better entitled, and better qualified, to hold.

"Could he, without embarrassment to you . . . go into your Military family," Lincoln suggested, "with some nominal rank, I, and not the public, furnishing his necessary means?" Grant promptly replied that he would be "most happy to have him" on his staff and would assign him the rank of Captain. Lincoln would not have to pay a cent.

Lincoln and Tad posed for the camera together for the final time on February 5, 1865. The father was much thinner after four grueling years of war, but the little boy was clearly growing up.

At last, on February 11, 1865, just one day before Lincoln's fifty-sixth and final birthday, his eldest son joined the Union army as an officer and left home for the front. Just a week earlier, Lincoln had taken not Bob but Tad for another sitting at a Washington photo gallery. One more time, father and son posed together before the cameras. The president looked thinner than ever, but for the first time in a photograph, managed a slight smile. Tad, wearing a gold watch chain that matched his father's, looked healthy and happy. Once again, Lincoln clutched a large book to pose alongside his little boy. But this time, almost as if he had now given up trying to teach the child to read, the book remained closed.

The following month, on a cloudy and drizzly late-winter day, Lincoln took the oath of office as president for the second time. The date was March 4, 1865.

Again, the great orator rose to the occasion for one last grand speech. Lincoln himself thought it the best of his career. To a vast throng of both blacks and whites, he sternly declared that, in some ways, all Americans, North as well as South, deserved the war's terrible suffering. It was because for so long they had all tolerated the sin of slavery. Then the president ended his sermonlike oration on a note of peace. As he concluded, the sun burst from the clouds, sending a thrill through the entire crowd:

"With malice toward none; with charity for all; with firmness in the right, as God gives us to see the right, let us strive on to finish the work we are in; to bind up the nation's wounds; to care for him who shall have borne the battle, and for his widow, and his orphan—to do all which may achieve and cherish a just, and a lasting peace, among ourselves, and with all nations."

Lincoln's second inauguration took place on an overcast March 4, 1865. As he began delivering his inaugural address, the sun suddenly burst through the clouds, thrilling the large crowd. The president regarded the speech he gave that day as the best of his career. He is standing behind the small podium, holding his speech.

Tad Lincoln astride his pony on the White House grounds during the Civil War. The tents in the background housed soldiers camped outside the presidential mansion.

Back in Washington for the inauguration, Bob showed off not only his spruce new uniform but his new friend—a young lady—and all of Washington took note. She was Mary Eunice Harlan, the daughter of a Republican senator from Iowa. Both the president and his wife seemed enormously pleased with their son's first serious girlfriend. They were pleased, too, by the progress that his commander, General Grant, was finally making in Virginia toward crushing Lee's army and bringing the long war to a close. And the Lincolns decided they wanted to be there to watch Grant do so.

Before they could leave the city, Tad, as so often before, befriended one more visitor to Washington—and the result was yet another image for history. This time the visitor was not a widow or soldier but one Henry F. Warren, a Massachusetts photographer. Warren all but ambushed the boy on the street one day and took a picture of him astride his pony. When he brought the finished print to the White House, Tad declared that he loved the photo. In return, Warren said: "Now bring out your father and I will make a picture of him for you." Moments later, Tad led an irritated Lincoln onto the windy White House balcony, where Warren had set up his camera.

Looking highly annoyed, the president submitted, squinting into the sun, as he sat still for the picture. No one ever thought it would be his last. (See page 230.)

Later in that month of March, Lincoln, Mary, and Tad headed off to visit Grant's army headquarters in Virginia. Feeling revived by the boat voyage, Lincoln remained with the troops for a total of eighteen days, the longest time he had ever stayed away from Washington as president. At Grant's headquarters, mother, father, and little brother were able to see Bob again. The president took the opportunity to meet with military leaders about how to end the fighting.

Unfortunately, the fighting was not limited to the battlefield. One day, Mary was observed flying into a jealous rage when she thought her husband was paying too much attention to a general's wife while visiting an army camp. A humiliated First Lady soon returned alone to the capital. But she quickly found she missed "Taddie very much." And when she heard that her husband had spent four or five hours with Captain Robert T. Lincoln (the president wired home that Bob was "well & in good spirits"), Mary decided to swallow her pride and ask to return. She still desired to be in Virginia to share the sweet moment of victory with her husband and sons.

Lincoln was sympathetic. "Tad and I are both well," he telegraphed her, "and will be glad to see you and your party here at the time you name." For her return visit, Mrs. Lincoln's "party" was much larger. Among the group was Bob's girlfriend, Mary Harlan (accompanied by her senator father). The First Lady knew that both young Mary and Bob would appreciate a reunion.

Meanwhile, Tad was having the time of his life. He got to spend time with his father, sleep aboard ship, visit soldiers and campsites, and occasionally even hear the rumble of real cannon fire in the distance. There was drama on this voyage, and fun, too. One lazy afternoon, the president spied a terrapin—a huge turtle—sunning himself on shore, and took Tad to watch the strange creature crawling clumsily along the rocks and mud.

Then on April 4, Tad's twelfth birthday, he joined his father for their greatest adventure yet: a surprise visit by boat to Richmond. For four years, this Virginia city had been the capital of the Confederacy. Now the Rebel government had fled, setting fire to much of the town, after which Union forces moved in to occupy it. Guarded by only a few sailors, Lincoln arrived there on a sweltering day, grasping Tad's hand as he stepped ashore. There the boy got to witness an extraordinary event.

Lincoln and Tad quietly visited the captured Confederate capital of Richmond, Virginia, on April 4, 1865—Tad's twelfth birthday. As the boy clutched his father's hand tightly, the city's newly freed slaves joyously surrounded their emancipator, cheering him wildly. This is how two artists of the day portrayed that unforgettable scene.

On the riverbank, a group of black laborers had been toiling in the hot sun. After Lincoln's army had marched into Richmond, these workers all became free men. And here suddenly, unexpectedly, came a familiar-looking visitor. It was hard to mistake the towering, bearded figure in the black suit and stovepipe hat. It was the proclamation's author, Lincoln himself, now strolling slowly toward them up the hill! Just to make sure the crowd knew who was approaching, a newspaper reporter on the scene let the people know it was the Great Emancipator himself.

With tears and shouts of joy, the ex-slaves rushed to his side and surrounded the president lovingly, declaring: "Bless the Lord . . . there is the great Messiah! Glory, Hallelujah." When one grateful old man fell to his knees in gratitude, Lincoln's voice trembled with emotion as he told him: "Don't kneel to me, that is not right. You must kneel to God only, and thank him for the liberty you will hereafter enjoy." Within minutes the streets were filled with other exuberant African Americans, "tumbling and shouting, from over the hills and from the water-side" to see up close the man they believed had freed them from their bondage.

Followed along the deserted streets by this excited crowd of black admirers, Lincoln and Tad strolled on toward Jefferson Davis's now-abandoned presidential mansion. There, Davis's own son, like Lincoln's, had died a few years earlier. Later, Lincoln and Tad took a long carriage ride through the city and visited the famous old Virginia capitol building, designed by one of the president's old heroes, Thomas Jefferson. (Today, a life-size statue of Lincoln and Tad sits near where this extraordinary day began, outside an old factory where the Confederacy once made the cannons to use against the Union. Father and son are portrayed here in bronze, seated next to each other on a bench. There is plenty of room for visitors to sit beside them and ponder Abraham and Tad Lincoln's unforgettable tour back in April 1865.) It was probably the proudest day of Tad's life—and his father's.

On April 9, just five days afterward, as Lincoln, Mary, and Tad were steaming by riverboat back to Washington, Lincoln learned with great joy that Robert E. Lee had finally surrendered his army to Ulysses S. Grant at a Virginia town called Appomattox. The war was finally ended. This time, Bob had been the one member of the Lincoln family who witnessed history. He was on the scene when General Lee rode up to a farmhouse to meet General Grant and sign the surrender papers. When the glorious news reached Washington, D.C., the entire city erupted in wild

Despite the war and their family tragedies, President and Mrs. Lincoln entertained often in the East Room of the White House. This is an artist's idea of how one of their parties might have looked. It was published in early 1865, just before Lincoln's assassination.

celebrations. Church bells rang, and music blared. Men marched through the streets cheering.

When happy crowds massed at the White House the following night to serenade their president, his youngest boy was still at his side. As one newspaper reported: "Master Tad Lincoln, who was at the window, appeared to hugely enjoy the shouting, cheering, and swaying to and fro of the crowd." White House guard W. H. Crook reported that "Tad was so excited he couldn't keep still." Then, "with a great shout of applause," wrote another reporter, "the young hopeful of the house of Lincoln" began waving a Confederate flag—just as he had done so naughtily four years earlier when the war was just beginning. Very likely, Tad had now unfurled a captured Rebel flag that soldiers in Virginia had handed Lincoln as a trophy during his recent tour. To the "uproarious cheers" of the crowd watching from below, Tad "was lugged back by the slack of his trowsers" by a servant.

At one point that happy night, Lincoln grew a bit mischievous himself. He asked the band to play "Dixie," the unofficial anthem of the Confederacy. After all, joked the president, the Union had "fairly captured" the tune as a "lawful prize" of war. Thinner and grayer than ever, Lincoln nonetheless seemed more cheerful than he had been in years. But as always, his boy's happiness came first. Ever thoughtful, he promptly wrote the secretary of war: "Tad wants some flags. Can he be accommodated?" And to Secretary of the Navy Gideon Welles, he sent a similar request for a keepsake: "Let Master Tad have a Navy sword."

Two nights after that, on April 11, the president appeared at a second-floor window of the White House to deliver a long, formal speech to a crowd gathered on the lawn below. His subject was a pressing one: the future of the long-divided country. For the first time he mentioned the idea of giving African Americans the right to vote—some of them, at least: the "very intelligent" and "those who serve our cause as soldiers."

The idea shocked some in the audience. One listener reacted with particular rage. He hated black people and believed the president would now try to make them American citizens for the first time. Turning to the man standing next to him, he hissed: "That is the last speech he will ever make. By God, I'll put him through." The man's name was John Wilkes Booth.

As Lincoln went on speaking that night, he dropped the pages of his handwritten manuscript to the floor, one by one, as he finished each sheet and

Captain Robert Lincoln brought this small picture of defeated Confederate commander Robert E. Lee home from Virginia in April 1865. Though he served as an officer on General Grant's staff for only a few months, Robert got to witness Lee's surrender at Appomattox. He showed this photo to his father on the very morning of the assassination.

turned to the next. Excited to be part of another historic moment, Tad crouched below, out of sight, and dutifully caught each piece of paper as it floated down in his direction. Working hard to keep the pages in order, he could be heard by some repeatedly whispering to his father: "Come, give me another!"

Yet when Lincoln had read every last page of his long text, someone in the crowd evidently thought that the president had failed to answer a crucial question. A loud voice was heard, demanding to know: "What shall we do with the rebels?"

"Hang them!" someone else in the crowd shouted. But crouching below the window, Tad answered back: "No, no, papa. Not hang them. Hang on to them!" And his father proudly cried out to the crowd: "That's it—Tad has got it. We must hang on to them!"

Three days later, on April 14, Bob returned safely to Washington and joined his excited, grateful family for an 8:00 a.m. breakfast. Both father and son had brought home souvenirs to show off from their recent, unforgettable experiences in Virginia. Lincoln had collected a handful of now-worthless Confederate money in Richmond. He had placed the bills in his wallet and brought them back to the White House.

Bob brought along a small photograph of General Lee, which he now took out to show his curious father. So here was the man who had kept Union armies in the thick of battle for so long! Lee's white beard made him look almost harmless. Lincoln studied the picture carefully. Then he solemnly said, "It is a good face; it is the face of a noble, noble, brave man. I am glad that the war is over at last."

He and Mary were planning to celebrate with a visit to nearby Ford's Theatre that very night. The president had long loved seeing plays. Appearing onstage tonight would be the famous English actress Laura Keene. Perhaps General and Mrs. Grant would attend as well (though in the end, they did not). And the president hoped Bob would join the party, too. But his son was exhausted and perhaps preferred to amuse himself with people his own age on his first night home from the war. He asked to be excused. Bob would never see his father alive again.

All that day, Lincoln worked as hard as ever, just as if a battle were raging somewhere. He saw important visitors, wrote notes and letters, strolled over to the War Department telegraph office to get the latest news from the army, and hosted a cabinet meeting with General Grant in attendance as a special guest. Most of all, he thought carefully about what he would do next as president to heal the wounds left by four years of war. He knew the country faced years of rebuilding. Cities lay in ruins, families had been divided, a million slaves were free, and six hundred thousand young men were dead, North and South.

In late afternoon, Mary convinced him to take a break and join her on a carriage ride. Together they headed down Pennsylvania Avenue. They drove past the shiny new Capitol dome, finally nearing completion after years of construction. Then they rode off to the river and paid a call on the Washington Navy Yard. There they inspected some recently damaged ironclad warships and greeted the officers and crew. That afternoon, husband and wife talked happily about their future. Perhaps they would travel to California someday. Maybe even as far as the Holy Land. "We must *both*, be more cheerful in the future," Mary remembered her husband telling her that day. "[B]etween the war & the loss of our darling Willie— we have both, been very miserable."

Returning to the White House between 6:00 and 7:00 p.m., they ate a light supper and then dressed for the theater. Tad headed off with a White House guard to see a play of his own. Like his parents, he loved seeing actors perform onstage and had joined his father at several plays over the past four years. Occasionally, the little boy had even appeared in costume as a guest performer, to Lincoln's immense delight. Remembered an eyewitness to one such surprise during the play *Pocahontas*: "The pleasure, the affection of the father was so intense, so spontaneous . . . it was glorious to see him." On this mid-April night, the boy would be attending the nearby National Theatre to see a play called *Aladdin, or The Wonderful Lamp*. White House doorkeeper Alphonso Donn, a favorite of the boy, would accompany him.

Ford's Theatre was draped in black after Abraham Lincoln was shot there on Good Friday, April 14, 1865. After the president's death, many angry citizens wanted this building torn down. But it survives to this day, housing both a theater and, in its basement, a Lincoln museum. There, the gun used to kill him is on display.

Lincoln still had a few more tasks to finish before he could take Mary out for the evening. Not surprisingly, his endless toil made them late. They did not arrive at Ford's Theatre, six blocks from the White House, until 8:30, after the play had started. But as the president and his wife made their way around the second-floor balcony to take their seats in a private box above the stage, the audience rose in applause. The actors stopped in midsentence, and the orchestra serenaded Lincoln with "Hail to the Chief." The tall, haggard president bowed to the adoring crowd and then took his seat in a rocking chair placed there especially for his comfort.

Holding hands with Mary, he settled in to watch the play, an English comedy called *Our American Cousin*. Along with the audience, Lincoln could soon be seen laughing heartily at its funniest lines.

Shortly after 10:00 p.m., the famous actor John Wilkes Booth—the man who had threatened Lincoln from the White House lawn during his most recent speech—stole into the packed theater. No one in the audience knew that, for months, he had been planning to kidnap Lincoln. Since Lee's surrender, his thoughts had turned instead to murder.

As the play continued, Booth snaked his way around the same balcony through which the Lincolns had strolled earlier. But no one seemed to notice him. All eyes remained focused on the stage—and the evening's honored guest. Silently, Booth tiptoed into the president's private box and then aimed a small handgun at the back of his head. Suddenly, the audience heard a loud cracking noise—followed by an explosion of smoke. Some members of the audience thought it was part of the play. That is, until Mary Lincoln began screaming for help. Her husband was slumped in his chair and would not respond to her. In the pandemonium, Booth leaped down to the stage and escaped.

Many in the audience panicked, but two doctors who happened to be at the play rushed into the presidential box and quickly examined the stricken leader. They were certain that Lincoln could not survive his massive injury. He was all but dead already. He would never recover.

But it was Good Friday. Those around him did not want the president to die inside a theater on such a holy day. So they carried his limp body downstairs and across the street to the boarding house owned by one William Petersen. There, Lincoln was tenderly placed in its tiny back bedroom. His frame was too long for its ordinary-size bed. Here he would spend the final nine hours of his life, never again speaking or opening his eyes, as the most famous men in Washington passed through the room to pay their final respects.

Sobbing hysterically, Mary Lincoln called desperately for her children. Bob, fast asleep at the White House, was awakened with the shocking news and brought quickly to the scene. For the rest of that terrible night and on into the next morning, he stood at his father's bedside. When Bob first saw his father's body, he gave vent to "his terrible grief" with loud sobs. Even after recovering, he continued quietly weeping for hours, holding a white handkerchief to dab his eyes. There was

Although neither artists nor photographers were on hand to record the Lincoln assassination, many rushed out imaginary and inaccurate scenes like this one anyway. For years, Lincoln admirers decorated their homes with such pictures.

nothing he could do—except blame himself for refusing to go to Ford's Theatre that night with his parents. For the rest of his life, Robert Lincoln would continue believing that had he been there he might have been able to save his father's life.

Panicked and distraught, Mary could not believe what was happening. Frantically trying to save her husband, she became convinced that if Tad were brought to his bedside, Lincoln would awaken and "speak to him because he loved him so." Thus for one last time, Mary painfully reminded Robert—and every other witness inside that tiny room—that he was not his father's favorite child.

Tad had been enjoying *Aladdin* when someone burst into the National Theatre to announce that the president had been shot. Some members of the audience suspected at first that it was a trick to cause panic so pickpockets could steal money in the confusion. That is, until a small boy was heard screaming and then seen rushing in a blur toward the back of the house and into the street. It was, of course, Tad. Doorkeeper Donn sped the boy back to the White House. There, Lincoln's youngest son saw one of his favorite guards, Thomas Pendel, and cried out for him, in a jumble of words harder to understand than ever: "O Tom Pen! o Tom Pen! They have killed Papa day! They've killed Papa day." Pendel comforted the child, cradling him in his arms in bed until he drifted off to a tearful sleep.

Back at the Petersen house, members of Lincoln's cabinet and staff now crowded into the tiny bedroom. Mary acted as if no one else were there, crying and shrieking at the top of her voice or moaning over and over again: "Why didn't he shoot me? Why didn't he shoot me?" At one point, frightened by a sudden rattling sound coming from her husband as he struggled to breathe, she screamed loudly, swooned, and collapsed with a thud to the floor. Secretary of War Stanton was so unnerved that he ordered that she be taken out of the room and not allowed back. Bob did nothing to counter Stanton's instructions—even if it meant that his mother would not be present

Lincoln died in the back bedroom of this modest-looking boarding house opposite Ford's Theatre on the rainy morning of April 15, 1865, nine hours after being shot by John Wilkes Booth. During the president's final hours, hundreds of Washington residents gathered silently on the street outside. The building still stands and is open to visitors.

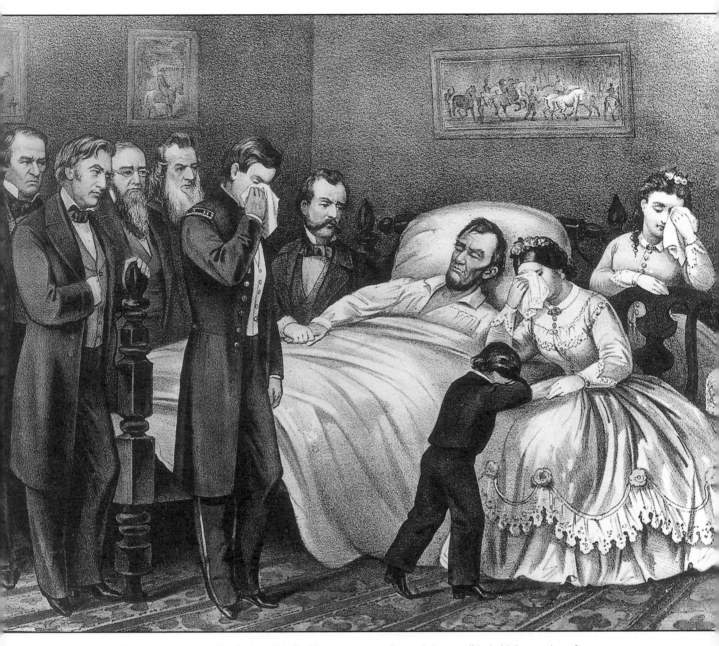

The bedroom where Lincoln spent his final hours was actually much too small to hold the number of eyewitnesses shown in this scene. But Americans wanted to believe that their great leader had died surrounded by friends, family, and colleagues. Mary, seen here, was actually in a nearby parlor, not at the bedside, when her husband breathed his last. Tad, shown crying on his mother's lap, was never there. He remained in the White House and never visited his father's deathbed.

when the president breathed his last. All Bob could find the strength to do was crouch in front of her and beg her: "Mother, please put your trust in God and all will be well." But Mary Lincoln had heard such assurances before. This time the pain was too much to bear. Just like Eddy and Willie, her precious husband—and God—were now abandoning her.

All through the long night, Lincoln lingered on, half-dead, half-alive, blood oozing onto his pillow, as doctors waited helplessly for the end to come. Outside, a drizzle began falling. When the sun came up, hundreds of anxious people could be seen in the street outside, huddled below the windows and crowded under umbrellas, waiting for news. At 7:22 a.m., Abraham Lincoln's great heart finally stopped beating. The sixteenth president of the United States—the author of the Emancipation Proclamation—the man who had won the Civil War and saved the Union—and the father of two surviving boys—was dead.

Later that gloomy morning, a company of soldiers brought Lincoln's body back to the quiet White House. When Secretary of the Navy Gideon Welles and Attorney General James Speed followed their chief inside, they caught sight of a bereft little boy standing by the first-floor window. He was staring out at the hundreds of African Americans who were gathered outside "weeping and wailing [at] their loss." The impish grin for which the boy was so well known was now erased from his face.

Tad Lincoln turned around and spoke just seven heartbreaking words: "Oh, Mr. Welles, who killed my father?" Welles and Speed were too overcome with sadness to offer a reply. They simply began to weep as well.

Lincoln's youngest boy seemed to age ten years in ten hours. To his nurse, the little boy soon remarked, "Pa is dead. I can hardly believe that I shall never see him again. I must learn to take care of myself now."

Then he looked up and added: "I am only Tad Lincoln now, little Tad, like other little boys. I am not a President's son now. I won't have many presents any more. Well, I will try and be a good boy, and will hope to go some day to Pa and brother Willie, in heaven."

Lincoln was honored in city after city along the long route home to Illinois. His funerals attracted hundreds of thousands of mourners. Here his coffin rides in a procession through the streets of Indianapolis, Indiana.

CHAPTER FIFTEEN
Fatherless

—◆—

Mary Lincoln returned to the White House that horrible morning, staggered to her bed, and remained there for weeks, unable to face outsiders, curtains drawn on the darkened room. She sobbed so continuously that at one point Tad begged her, "Don't cry so, Mamma! don't cry, or you will make me cry, too! You will break my heart." But try as she did to calm herself for Tad's sake, she was powerless to stop her shrieking and crying. Late one night, her "terrible outbursts" woke the little boy, and he crept into her room in his nightshirt and pleaded again: "Don't cry, Mamma; I cannot sleep if you cry! Papa was good, and he has gone to heaven. He is happy there."

But "Papa"'s other survivors were miserable. Recalling Mary's solitary grief when Willie died three years earlier, few people were surprised when Mary proved unable to rouse herself to attend her husband's funeral. It took place in the East Room of the White House—where they had hosted so many parties in the past.

One observer reported that Tad joined his brother and six hundred other mourners for the solemn prayer service there, the littlest Lincoln sobbing "as if his heart would break." But most witnesses maintained that Bob was in fact the only Lincoln in attendance. Still, the youngest member of the shattered Lincoln family remained very much on the public mind. The longtime object of curiosity—and sometimes of resentment as well—was now an object of sympathy.

Within weeks, a composer had written a sad new tune to express the sorrow of the country as well as of the child. The song "Little Tad" became a national favorite:

God bless the little orphan boy! A father's darling pride.
May heaven guard his youthful form. And be his hope and guide.
May that pure love and honest worth which fill'd his parent's heart
Be his inheritance in life. The good and gen'rous part.

But yet there's left a mother's love to watch his youthful years.
For them a nation's sympathy. For them a nation's tears.
Columbia never can forget the kindred of her Friend.
And for the little orphan boy o'er will her love extend.

On the days that followed Lincoln's assassination, all of Washington seemed to crowd the streets to pay tribute to the dead president. Then, on Friday morning, April 21, en route to the train station on the other end of town, a carriage bearing his remains rolled slowly past buildings now draped in black. Thousands looked on silently as the sad parade passed by, their hats lifted in one final show of love and respect.

Lincoln would go home to Springfield now—to be buried. Not one but two Lincoln sons would join him for the journey: Bob, of course, but also Willie. The dead child's coffin was now gently lifted from its Georgetown cemetery vault and placed in the railroad car taking his father on his final trip. It would be the 1861 inaugural journey in reverse: a trip of 1,600 miles north and west, with tributes in many cities along the route. But this time there would be no cheers, no speeches—only public viewings of Lincoln's body and large funerals attended by hoards of admirers. All along the route would come the sound of muffled drums and sorrowful music.

On May 4, with Bob alone still representing his family, Abraham Lincoln was laid to rest in a temporary vault at Oak Ridge Cemetery in Springfield. "My heart ached for him," a cousin who glimpsed Bob there admitted, "he seemed to feel so sadly." Mary did not visit the cemetery until winter. Not for another six years would a large tomb rise on the hill above the vault. There, Lincoln would finally be laid to rest permanently. And there he lies today.

Back home in Springfield, Illinois, the Lincoln family's old house—now rented to a railroad executive—was draped in black as a sign of the city's respect and sadness.

Not until May 23, 1865, more than two weeks after her husband's burial, did Mary Lincoln finally summon the strength to leave her room and move out of the White House at last. Though it took her more than a month to yield the mansion to the new president, Andrew Johnson, she later claimed: "Bidding Adieu, to *that house*, would *never* have troubled me, if . . . I had carried with me, the loved ones, who entered the house, with me." But of course, she could not do so. Lincoln and Willie were gone. Bob had grown up. Mrs. Keckly and two White House guards were now her sole companions. She still had Tad, of course. But in her grief, she insisted, "Alas, all is over with me."

Mary's worry now was over not just loneliness—but money. Surprisingly, her lawyer husband had left no last will. Lincoln had saved almost all of his large presidential salary. Nearly eighty-five thousand dollars was left in all, and Congress

Now in charge of his shattered family, twenty-two-year-old Robert grew a moustache after his father's death to make himself look older.

generously awarded him the full amount he would have earned had he lived through 1865. But unlike today, a president's widow received no government pension. Even after the president's estate was divided equally among his heirs—one-third each to Mary, Bob, and Tad—Mrs. Lincoln convinced herself that she was poor. For the rest of her tragic life, Mary was haunted by manic fears that she would run out of money and have no way to support herself.

Bob, who had returned to Washington after his father's burial, now escorted his mother and brother back to Illinois, but not to Springfield. Too many painful memories dwelled in her old hometown, and Mary could count on few friends there to comfort her. Instead, the reduced family moved into a fine Chicago hotel, then, when rates proved too expensive, to a three-room suite in a cheaper one.

Bob decided he could not leave his mother and Tad alone to return to Harvard Law School. So he began studying at a local law firm (just as his father had). By all accounts, he rose to these challenges, showing both affection and responsibility. He treated Mary with much tenderness and took charge of his father's letters and documents while working with lawyers to settle the president's estate. Yet Mary continued to bemoan the fact that God had deprived her boys "of their counsellor & protector."

Mary felt especially "humiliated" that the dead president's family should now be living in a boarding house. General Grant, she jealously noted, had been given free homes as gifts. Her family, on the other hand, had become what Mary called "Living Monuments of a Nation's ingratitude!" For a time, however, Mary tried to make the best of things. She proudly wrote to the boys' old White House tutor, Alexander Williamson, to report that Taddie's "lovely nature" had remained unchanged. And she admitted that "in our day of sorrow and adversity," Robert had shown himself "a youth of great nobleness."

Bob tried hard to conceal his own broken heart—which probably ached hardest over the knowledge that he would never get the chance to grow close at last to his father. "In all my plans for the future," he wrote to a Harvard professor, "the chief object I had in view was" his father's praise. "[N]ow that he is gone . . . I feel utterly without spirit or courage. I know that such a feeling is wrong, and that it is my duty to overcome it. I trust that for the sake of my Mother and little brother that I will be able to do so." For a time, Mary believed he succeeded. But their close relationship would not last.

Tad Lincoln, as he looked when he began living in Chicago with his mother after the assassination. Long the mischievous "sprite" of the White House, Tad seemed much more serious after his father's death.

Mary posed for this rare photo after her husband's murder. After 1865, she never again appeared in public wearing anything but black dresses and bonnets. She remained in official mourning for the rest of her life.

Bob soon concluded he would "almost as soon be dead" than remain in the "dreary" rooms together with his mother and brother. Mary herself admitted that the place was "revolting." So Bob moved into an apartment of his own. Though now living separately, Bob tried to make sure Tad finally began taking school seriously.

Mary hated parting with Tad, "even for a day." But by September she proudly told tutor Williamson that "Taddie is going to a school & for once in his life, he is really interested in his studies." Tad even offered to purchase his own copy of J. G. Holland's new biography of his father, though it is doubtful he would have been able to read it on his own. Mary tried to blame family tragedy for his lack of education. "After all," she believed, "few children learn well, without some one, sharing their lessons. If his darling, precious brother Willie had lived, *he* Tad would have been much further advanced." Mary tried to deal with Tad's longtime speech problems, too. She had him fitted with clumsy braces, but they made the boy harder to understand than ever. Bob finally ordered the painful braces removed, and brought in a speech therapist to treat his little brother.

By November of their first year alone, his mother was able to boast to painter Francis B. Carpenter: "Taddie is learning to be diligent in his studies." Typically, she gave no credit to Robert when reporting that Tad "appears to be rapidly making up, for the great amount of time, he lost in W[ashington]."

Mary had good reason for confiding in the artist. Carpenter had worked for six months in the White House in 1864 on a painting of Lincoln's cabinet, his "happy family" as Mary had once testily described it. But now, even though both the father and a son had died, the artist proposed a group portrait of the president with his *real* family (even if, in truth, *they* had seldom been happy at all): Abraham, Mary, Robert, Willie, and Tad. Mary embraced the idea, predicting that such a picture would be highly "prized." To help Carpenter along with his plan, she shared her favorite family photographs for the artist's use as models. She made sure the painter understood that Willie "was a very beautiful boy, with a most *spiritual* expression of face." Not surprisingly, she suggested that the artist copy a four-year-old picture of herself—one that made her look much thinner than she really was.

Not only did Francis Carpenter produce his group portrait of the Lincoln family, but it was then beautifully engraved so copies could be sold to the public. Many other artists produced similar prints. Soon many American families were displaying pictures of the Lincolns. These pictures typically showed them gathered together around a parlor table. The sad truth, of course, was that they had seldom enjoyed such occasions in real life. Willie had died during their first year in the White House. Bob was away at school. And Mary admitted she felt fortunate if her husband got to spend a few minutes talking to her after eleven o'clock at night.

But Lincoln admirers did not care about the reality. They wanted to remember the Lincolns as a united family. And they wanted to imagine that the dead president's wife and children had provided some comfort for him while he lived. The prim Bob, for one, thought such fakes dishonest, grumbling: "There was never such a group actually assembled."

In September 1868, Bob and Mary Harlan decided to get married in Washington. Naturally, the groom wanted what was left of his family to be at his side for the wedding. But Mary and Tad, who had been vacationing together in the Pennsylvania mountains, seemed almost reluctant to come. For one thing, Mary explained, Tad had "met some fine boys" there, not to mention "some young ladies," and appeared "very happy" at last. But if it was hard for Tad to leave the mountains, it was even more so for Mary, who feared showing her face again in the capital, even for her son's wedding. Although she admitted that "the terror of having to proceed to *Washington* to witness it, almost overpowers me," she managed to pull herself together and attend the ceremony and reception in Senator John Harlan's home.

Mary thought the "marriage passed off finely." She seemed especially pleased to see the "very rich" gifts the couple received from the thirty or so guests. The new Mary Lincoln wore white. The old one wore black. Robert sported a newly grown moustache. If the newlyweds looked tense that day, there was good reason. The groom had only recently warned his bride that his mother was likely to cause "a great deal of trouble in the future." Never did Bob speak truer words.

Fortunately for all concerned, Mary declined the newlyweds' more than generous invitation to join them on their honeymoon trip to New York. She claimed she felt too ill. But she allowed Tad to go along with the happy couple and traveled back alone. Before she left, Mary decided to make good use of her time back in Washington. She busied herself with her three-year-long campaign to win a government pension. In arguing her case, she wrote the Senate that she had earned such "care" as the sickly "widow of a President of the United States whose life was sacrificed to his country's service." But her claims of poverty and ruin still fell on deaf ears in the capital. Desperate, Mary caused a major public scandal by putting her old clothes on sale in New York. It was supposed to be a secret, but word leaked out to the press. Robert was mortified and angry.

Mary felt humiliated, too, blaming Elizabeth Keckly and ending their friendship. Worse, she convinced herself that Bob was mismanaging her money. Mary decided in late 1868 to flee the country altogether and live in Europe. Tad had been in and out of Chicago schools for three years. Mary had even thought of enrolling him at a boarding school in Racine, Wisconsin. But every time she thought too hard about little boys sleeping in a big, impersonal dormitory room without their mothers to care for them, she withdrew Tad from school. As far as we know, such thoughts had never crossed her mind about Bob.

Though fifteen-year-old Tad finally seemed to be growing up, even learning in school, his mother talked herself into believing that a major change would do him good, too. The pair sailed for Europe that fall and, by October 1868, reached distant Germany. There, Mary settled in Frankfurt and enrolled Tad in a boarding school known as Dr. Hohagen's Institute. Mary missed her "precious child Taddie" enormously.

She was still living in Germany when she learned to her delight that she had become a grandmother for the first time. "So, is he not, a young Papa?" she said of Robert. The new baby brought back sweet memories. "[I]t appears to me, at *times*, so short a time, since my darling husband, was bending over me, with such love and tenderness—when the young father of that babe—was born." The baby girl, who came into the world on October 15, 1869, was called Mary, too—though no one ever knew whether she was named for her mother or her grandmother. The new "grandmamma" thought the confusion might be "too much in the beginning." But for once she held her tongue. Grandmother Lincoln would not see the newest Mary—soon known as "Mamie"—until the baby was nearly two years old.

Meanwhile, the Franco-Prussian War broke out on the Continent, and Mary and Tad were forced to move yet again, this time to England, where Tad continued his education with a new private tutor. In July 1870, after five years of Mary's pleading, Congress at last granted her an annual pension—not the five thousand dollars a year she hoped for, but the still-generous sum of three thousand dollars.

As Christmas approached, Tad begged his mother to take him home to America

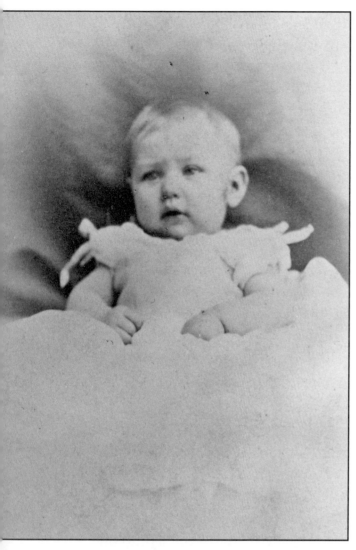

Baby Mary Lincoln (1869–1938)—nicknamed "Mamie"—was the first grandchild of the slain president. Grandmother Mary believed the infant was named for her, but the baby may have been named after Robert's wife, also named Mary.

for the holidays. He missed his brother and wanted to meet his new niece. "Tad is almost wild to see Bob, you, and the Baby," Mary wrote her daughter-in-law. But, worried that a winter sea voyage would expose her "beautiful, darling *good* boy to the elements, at this season of the year," she postponed their homecoming until the following spring. In May 1871, Mary and Tad together crossed the Atlantic and docked in New York. John Hay saw them there and was surprised to discover that Tad now spoke with a slight German accent. But he also found the once mischievous terror to be "modest and cordial." And Hay was simply astounded at how much the former chubby elf now looked like his father. New photographs confirmed Tad's sudden and striking resemblance to the late president.

Mother and son headed west to Chicago by train for their reunion with Robert, his wife, and their baby. But Mary's worst fears soon came to pass. The sea voyage had sapped Tad's strength. Just as his mother had worried, he had caught a severe cold on board ship, and it would not go away. Doctors in Chicago told his distraught mother that water was slowly filling his lungs and choking him. Tad soon spiked a fever and began suffering chest pain. Medical experts believed he had developed pneumonia, but it is probable he had come down with a case of incurable tuberculosis. His lungs became so congested that he was soon unable to sleep unless strapped upright in a chair. "His mother," reported an old family friend, was "in great affliction."

Mary's hopes rose briefly in mid-July when Tad's health suddenly improved. But his recovery proved temporary. Just a few days later, his lungs grew full again. His legs began to swell and his skin turned blue. Early on the morning of July 15, 1871, eighteen-year-old Thomas "Tad" Lincoln died, still sitting in the chair in which he had spent the last painful month of his life. For once, Mary somehow found the strength to attend a family member's funeral, sitting in shocked despair for a service at Robert's house. But she firmly believed: "There is no life for me, without my idolized Taddie." How much could a mother suffer?

This was perhaps the cruelest blow of all. "As grievous as other bereavements have been," Mary wrote to a woman she had met while vacationing with Tad a few years earlier, "not one great sorrow, ever approached the agony of *this*. My idolized & devoted son, torn from me, when he had blossomed into such a noble, promising youth."

Robert accompanied his brother's body to Oak Ridge Cemetery, where Tad joined Abraham, Eddy, and Willie Lincoln at rest. At last, as writer Ruth Painter Randall

Tad Lincoln—even with a fake moustache penciled in to make him appear mature—had begun to look much like his late father by the time this picture was taken after he and his mother returned from Europe. The photo probably dates to around 1871, the year of Tad's death.

observed in her book *Lincoln's Sons*, Tad was again sleeping peacefully beside his beloved father, just as he had done so often as a small boy in the White House.

⸻ ❈ ⸻

Tad's tragic death should have brought the mother and her last living son closer together. But instead, it drove them farther apart. Mary was more demanding than ever. And Robert was exhausted from the years of caring for his mother and brother—worrying about their lives or, some whispered, trying to control them. He wanted peace. He had a family of his own to support.

It did not help matters that Mary began, at least in Bob's opinion, to lose her reason. The latest family tragedy, her son believed, had affected not only her spirit but her mind. Mary fled briefly to Florida, but then rushed home after imagining that Robert, too, was dying. She caused such trouble in her son's home that, for a time, Robert's wife moved out.

It was Robert's mother who left instead, saving her son's marriage but ending any chance they would ever again be close. Resuming her wandering, Mary traveled throughout the country. One day, she found herself in the Boston gallery of a faker named William Mumler. He described himself as a "spirit photographer." Desperate and gullible, Mary allowed herself to believe Mumler could somehow produce a picture of her together with her dead husband's ghost. The old woman posed alone in his studio, looking small and vulnerable. Of course, the final photo was altered. The print Mumler handed to Mary showed two ghostly forms standing behind her: a bearded man (his hands lovingly on her shoulders) and a young boy.

Mumler's wife, a medium, claimed she heard a voice trying to send Mary a message identifying these figures: "Mother, if you cannot recognize father, show the picture to Robert; he will recognize it." With mounting excitement, Mary asked who was speaking. Mrs. Mumler claimed it was Tad, although she used the wrong name, "Thaddeus," which should have alerted Mary to the scam. More than satisfied, Mary clutched the fake photo and treasured it. Photographer Mumler eventually went on trial for fraud.

By 1875, lonelier than ever, Mary was back living in a Chicago hotel, taking drugs to help her sleep, hiding her money in her underwear, and, some complained, wandering the hallways half-dressed, imagining that strangers were following her

Looking far older than her years, Mary Todd Lincoln sat for this, her last photograph, around 1875, the year Robert put her on trial for insanity. Created by a "spirit photographer" in Boston, it supposedly showed the ghosts of Lincoln and Tad comforting her in the background. The photographer was later put on trial for fakery.

or pulling wires in her head. Mary had explanations for all her odd behavior, but her son no longer listened. He now had two more children to care for: Two-year-old Abraham Lincoln II, known as "Jack," and a new baby girl, Jessie. Robert feared for his mother's safety, not to mention her fortune, but most of all feared public embarrassment. Facing the most difficult choice of his entire life, he decided to seek psychiatric help for his tortured mother—whether she wanted treatment or not.

The state of Illinois boasted unusually liberal laws where insanity was concerned. Men could not simply commit women to institutions without a public trial. But a public court hearing would certainly humiliate the onetime First Lady. Nevertheless, in May Mary was brought, without warning and against her will, to a Chicago courtroom and placed on trial. Angry but dazed, with no time to prepare a real defense, she sat by meekly as the jury heard so-called evidence that she had lost her mind. She was spending money wildly. She was seeing visions, hearing noises. She could no longer care for herself safely. In fact, she might well do herself harm. The jury took but ten minutes to convict Mary Lincoln of insanity and commit her to an asylum in Batavia, Illinois, some forty miles from Chicago. During the trial, Robert tried reaching for her hand, but Mary refused to take it. "Oh, Robert," she cried, "to think that my son would do this to me."

Mary spent months in confinement—though of a privileged sort. Doctors and nurses treated her royally, assigning her to a suite and inviting her to take meals with the owners. Robert visited her faithfully. Mary did grow calmer—perhaps helped along by drugs. She even tried to be pleasant to Robert. In September her doctors permitted her to leave the asylum and travel down to Springfield to live with her sister, Elizabeth Edwards. Ten years after her husband's death, thirty-four years after their wedding inside this very house, a small, overweight, elderly looking lady in black came back to the scene of her happiest day. But if Robert thought she would now stay quiet, content to remain an outpatient with a conviction for insanity on her record, he would soon learn otherwise.

For weeks, Mary had been secretly working with a husband-and-wife team of lawyers to regain her official freedom—and control over her own money. Her careful planning and strong determination suggest that if she was ever truly insane, she had now recovered. At a second trial in Chicago, a new jury agreed. On June 15, 1876, Mary Lincoln was ruled sane and officially set free.

The decree also freed Mary to say what she really felt to the son she believed had plotted against her. She no longer had to pretend to be pleasant just to gain her liberty. Just four days after her release, she wrote a brutal letter to her only surviving child. She wanted all her possessions back, whether they were gifts, loans, or property she believed Bob and his wife had stolen from her:

"Robert T. Lincoln," she began with icy formality. "Do not fail to send me without *the least* delay, *all* my paintings . . . my silver set with large silver waiter . . . my silver tête-à-tête set also other articles your wife appropriated and which are *well known* to you, must be sent, without a day's delay. . . . Send me my laces, my diamonds, my jewelry—My unmade silks, white lace dress—double lace shawl & flounce, lace scarf: and other goods," including books. The list went on and on. And then Mary furiously concluded: "Two prominent clergymen, have written me, since I saw you, and mention in their letters, that they think it advisable to offer prayers for you in Church, on account of your wickedness against me and High Heaven. . . . You have injured yourself, not me, by your wicked conduct."

Miserable but ever-defiant, Mary left America again for yet another long exile, this time in France. "God, can *alone*, lighten the burden, until I am reunited to my dearly beloved husband, and children," she wrote her sister from the French town of Pau in March 1877. "But waiting," she told a friend, "is so long."

Meanwhile, she cut off all contact with her only surviving son—whom she now dismissed as a "wretched young man, but *old* in sin." The boy she had once praised as her "good" child now became in her eyes "a monster of mankind." She firmly believed that God would never allow Bob to see his father in heaven "on account of his heartless cruelty, to the wife of a man who worshipped me." Her only personal correspondence went either to a Springfield banker or a young nephew. "I have been called upon to surrender—two, of the loveliest sons, that God ever gave to a Mother," she said in one of these long letters, ". . . and for whom I shall never cease to grieve, with an almost unparalleled sorrow, until God reunites us." Not until the fall of 1880 did she finally decide to return to America.

A reporter waiting for her ship on a New York dock—only because world-famous actress Sarah Bernhardt was on board, too—glimpsed the tiny figure as she limped down the gangplank. "Among the passengers," he alerted his readers, "was an aged lady; she was dressed plainly; her face was furrowed and her hair was streaked with white—this was the widow of Abraham Lincoln. She was almost unnoticed."

She was also terribly alone. Mary had nowhere else to go but back once more to Springfield. There, her merciful sister again took her in. Mary retreated to an upstairs room along with her dozens of trunks, all still overflowing with lace, gloves, shawls, and dresses—the goods she never wore but still loved to unfold and repack day after day.

One day in May 1881, after years cut off from her son and grandchildren, an unexpected visitor showed up at the Edwards home. It was the country's new secretary of war—none other than Robert T. Lincoln. To make sure he would be welcome, some say he brought along eleven-year-old Mamie. No one knows how the frail Mary reacted to this surprise. But Robert returned to Springfield believing that a new beginning was possible in their long-damaged relationship.

Though suspicious of Robert's sudden concern, and physically weak from diabetes and other ailments, Mary somehow found strength to launch one final fight for what she believed she deserved: more money from Congress. Even though she no longer had large expenses or a child to support, she insisted that her original pension was just too small. Determined to return to Washington to wage in person the battle for a raise, she got as far as New York, where she admitted to growing "very feeble with my spine & limbs." She could no longer walk more than a few steps without help and was nearly blind. Mary never made it to the capital, though Congress did vote her the increase for which she yearned.

In March 1882, confined now to a wheelchair, she somehow managed to survive the exhausting train trip back to Springfield. She spent the last four months of her life alone inside her sunless bedroom at the Edwards home. There, Mary Ann Todd Lincoln, mother of the Lincoln boys, died quietly on July 16, 1882. Though she looked far older, she was only sixty-three years old. The doctor listed the cause as "paralysis." Perhaps a stroke had finally freed her from her years of misery. Mary was entombed beside her husband and children at Oak Ridge.

The preacher at her funeral compared Abraham Lincoln and his wife to two great trees that had stood so long side by side that their roots grew tightly together, intertwined. Then one day a lightning bolt had killed one of the trees—just as John Wilkes Booth had killed the president. The stricken tree died immediately, but its companion lived on—or so it seemed. In reality, its roots had died with its partner's, and it slowly faded away. Much like Mary Lincoln.

Three of the four Lincoln boys were now gone—only one was left. Now a bearded statesman, Robert did well as secretary of war in James A. Garfield's cabinet—but had been horrified to find himself on the scene when an assassin fired the shots that killed yet another president. Once again, Robert Lincoln had played an unexpected, unwanted role in the drama of a presidential murder.

He continued serving as secretary of war, now under the new president, Chester Alan Arthur. Even in her final years, Bob's mother had dreamed that he might one day serve as president himself. Little Mamie, she fantasized, would certainly "grace" the White House. But whenever others began seriously considering the same idea, Robert put a stop to any hope that a second Lincoln might run for the nation's highest office. He saw nothing glamorous about the White House and found public life "morbid." As he admitted to a journalist, "It seems difficult for the average American to understand that it is possible for anyone not to desire the presidency, but I most certainly do not. I have seen too much of it."

Instead, in 1889, he took on the important post of American minister to the Court of St. James's in England. But tragedy and bad luck followed him all the way to London. There, a year later, his own son, the namesake of his famous father, died young, too. It was "the hardest of many hard things" that had occurred in his life, Robert told John Hay.

Then, sounding much like Abraham Lincoln had sounded when Willie died nearly three decades earlier, Robert said about his latest loss: "I did not realize until he was gone how deeply my thoughts of the future were in him."

Of all four of Abraham Lincoln's sons, only Robert lived into the twentieth century. Here he poses for a photographer at age seventy in 1913. He inscribed this picture to his granddaughter, Mary Lincoln Beckwith. Meeting him around this time, writer Ida Tarbell said he looked as if he was "just out of the barber's chair."

EPILOGUE
The End of the Story

Robert Lincoln remained at his post in London for three more years, retreating home in 1893 to America and to private life. No one could doubt that he had been a fine minister. He had represented his country well. He was popular among the British people. He once had even enjoyed a dinner with Queen Victoria herself. Even his presidential father had never met European royalty.

Robert returned to the practice of law with enormous success and became a railroad executive with the Pullman Company. He built his inheritance—originally from his father, then made larger after the death of Tad and their mother—into a multimillion-dollar fortune. He maintained fine homes in Washington and Chicago and built a summer mansion named Hildene in Manchester, Vermont, the mountainside village he had visited with his mother so many years before.

Although Republicans still floated his name as a presidential possibility in the years that followed, Robert always took himself out of the running. He was no longer in politics, though he made an exception when former president Theodore Roosevelt tried for a comeback in 1912. Robert hated Roosevelt even though T.R. was a great Lincoln admirer and had been served (like Lincoln) by John Hay. Roosevelt loved quoting Abraham Lincoln, which Robert found offensive. Republican president William Howard Taft was more to his taste, so he tried helping the rotund, conservative president win reelection by inviting him to Hildene for a round of golf. Even in the twentieth century, associating with a Lincoln was still valuable to politicians. Taft lost anyway, finishing third that year. The new president, Woodrow Wilson, began claiming inspiration from Lincoln, too—and he was a Democrat!

Through all these years, Robert continued to do what he believed a dutiful son must do to protect his father's memory—and preserve his mother's privacy.

He destroyed some of their personal letters, a great loss to history. But he lovingly cared for the president's official records. In fact, he guarded these so ferociously that they always went wherever he traveled—packed in trunks aboard a special railroad car.

Lincoln's aging son patiently answered writers' questions and helped his father's former secretaries, Nicolay and Hay, as they worked to produce an official biography of the Lincoln administration. But he was not above complaining when he did not like a particular new book, and he became especially furious at two of his father's longtime friends, Ward Hill Lamon and William Herndon, when they published memoirs he disliked. When the city of London, where he had served as minister, attempted to honor Abraham Lincoln with what Robert judged to be an undignified-looking statue by sculptor George Gray Barnard, Robert went into a fury. He mounted such a passionate campaign to stop the project that eventually the statue was replaced by a more formal one.

Otherwise, Robert rarely involved himself directly in tributes to his father. He did speak once, briefly, at an anniversary event at the site of one of the Lincoln-Douglas debates. He attended a one-hundredth birthday event for the late president in 1909, but refused an invitation to give a speech. He even survived long enough to join

President Warren G. Harding (left) and Congressman Joseph Cannon (right), a former Speaker of the House of Representatives, flank an elderly Robert Lincoln at the dedication of the Lincoln Memorial in Washington on May 30, 1922. Cannon, a great admirer of President Lincoln, thought the unpopular Robert was "one of the most misunderstood citizens of the country."

Robert Lincoln built this mansion in Manchester, Vermont, in 1905 and named it Hildene. He eventually took up residence here full time and died in the house in 1926.

President Warren G. Harding at the dedication of the Lincoln Memorial in Washington in 1922. But if that occasion—or that place—moved him in a special way, he kept his feelings to himself, as usual. He said nothing.

In his last years, he much preferred playing golf to giving interviews about the Civil War years. Robert wrote and said so little about his father during his long, long life that he left us with no real picture of their relationship. He became so determined to seek no special privileges as Abraham Lincoln's son that he instead closed the door on any chance that we would better understand his father—or, for that matter, himself.

Was he shy? Resentful? Noble? Oversensitive? Foolish? Heartless? It is still hard to know. Only one thing seems certain: from the beginning of his life to the end, this Lincoln was, as a Springfield observer had declared so long ago, "all Todd."

Robert became the only Lincoln child to live to adulthood, and he was also the first to live to old age. He was nearly eighty-three when he died in his sleep in 1926 in a bedroom that overlooked the garden at his beloved Vermont estate. Reporting his passing, a newspaper emphasized that Robert had always avoided living "in the

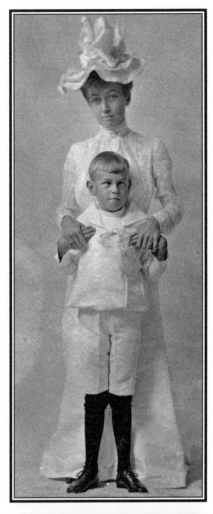

Robert Lincoln's daughter Mamie—Mary Isham—poses with her son Lincoln Isham (1892–1971), probably around the dawn of the twentieth century.

shadow of his father's greatness." Instead, he had tried to stand "on his own feet." The same, unfortunately, could not really be said of his children and grandchildren.

Robert's daughter Mamie grew up to marry and bear a child of her own. She named her son Lincoln—Lincoln Isham—but he did not carry the famous family name. Nor did he and his wife have children of their own.

Sister Jessie Lincoln had several husbands. She bore a daughter named Mary Todd Lincoln Beckwith, in honor of her grandmother, and who was known to her friends as "Peggy." Peggy remained single all her life and had no children. Her younger brother was called Robert Todd Lincoln Beckwith, but though he married several women, he never fathered a child. These great-grandchildren were the last living direct descendants of Abraham Lincoln.

The Beckwiths had plenty of family money to live their lives in comfort without developing careers of their own. Unlike Abraham Lincoln, they had no passion for politics and no devotion to public service. Nor did they appear to care very much about their celebrated ancestor. As Peggy admitted during the one-hundreth anniversary of the Civil War: "I'm as far away from him as anyone else." Peggy died

Lincoln Isham, Abraham Lincoln's great-grandson, as he looked in old age. Isham, who lived to age seventy-nine, had no children of his own.

in 1975, and her brother, Bob, in 1985. There would be no more descendants of the sixteenth president of the United States.

What might have happened had the other Lincoln boys lived to grow up and raise children of their own? The serious-minded Willie, so much like his father. Or the compassionate and humorous Tad, finally beginning to learn as he neared adulthood. Or, for that matter, Abraham Lincoln II—Jack—the president's only male grandchild, Bob's own beloved son, and the last hope for the Lincoln family name to live.

But, of course, Jack did not live. Like so many members of his family, he died too soon.

That is where this book began—and where the story of the Lincoln sons ends.

Robert's second daughter was Jessie Harlan Lincoln Beckwith (1875–1948). Here she poses with her children Mary (left) and Robert.

Brother and sister Robert Todd Lincoln Beckwith (1904–1985) and Mary Todd Lincoln Beckwith (1898–1975), known as "Peggy," never had children of their own. When they died, the Lincoln line ended forever.

BIBLIOGRAPHY

Angle, Paul M. *"Here I Have Lived": A History of Lincoln's Springfield, 1821–1865*. Chicago: Abraham Lincoln Book Shop, 1971. Originally published in 1950.

Anonymous. "The President's Son." *American Phrenological Journal* 35 (April 1862): 77.

Babcock, Bernie. *Lincoln's Mary and the Babies*. Philadelphia: J. B. Lippincott, 1929.

Baker, Jean H. *Mary Todd Lincoln: A Biography*. New York: W. W. Norton, 1987.

Basler, Roy P., ed. *The Collected Works of Abraham Lincoln*. 9 vols. New Brunswick, NJ: Rutgers University Press, 1953–1955.

Bayne, Julia Taft. *Tad Lincoln's Father*. Lincoln: University of Nebraska Press, 2001. Originally published in 1931.

Berry, Stephen. *House of Abraham: Lincoln and the Todds, A Family Divided by War*. Boston: Houghton Mifflin, 2007.

Bullard, F. Lauriston. *Tad and His Father*. Boston: Little, Brown, 1915.

Burlingame, Michael, ed. *Lincoln Observed: Civil War Dispatches of Noah Brooks*. Baltimore: Johns Hopkins University Press, 1998.

———, ed. *With Lincoln in the White House: Letters, Memoranda, and Other Writings of John G. Nicolay, 1860–1865*. Carbondale: Southern Illinois University Press, 2000.

Carpenter, Francis B. "Anecdotes and Reminiscences of President Lincoln." In *The Life, Public Services, and State Papers of Abraham Lincoln*, edited by Henry J. Raymond. New York: Derby and Miller, 1865.

———. *Six Months at the White House with Abraham Lincoln: The Story of a Picture*. New York: Hurd and Houghton, 1867.

Catton, Bruce. "Lincoln, as White House Nurse Saw Him." *DeKalb* (Illinois) *Chronicle*, February 12, 1931.

Crook, W[illiam]. H. *Memories of the White House*. Boston: Little, Brown, 1911.

Emerson, Jason. *The Madness of Mary Lincoln*. Carbondale: Southern Illinois University Press, 2007.

BIBLIOGRAPHY

Emery, Tom. *Eddie, Lincoln's Forgotten Son* (monograph). Carlinville, IL: History in Print, 2009.

Epstein, Daniel Mark. *The Lincolns: Portrait of a Marriage*. New York: Ballantine Books, 2008.

Fehrenbacher, Don E., and Virginia Fehrenbacher, eds. *Recollected Words of Abraham Lincoln*. Stanford, CA: Stanford University Press, 1996.

French, Benjamin Brown. *Witness to the Young Republic: A Yankee's Journal, 1828–1870*. Edited by Donald B. Cole and John J. McDonough. Hanover, NH: University Press of New England, 1989.

Glyndon, Howard. "The Truth About Mrs. Lincoln." *The Independent*, August 20, 1882, 3–5.

Goff, John S. *Robert Todd Lincoln: A Man in His Own Right*. Norman: University of Oklahoma Press, 1969.

Goodwin, Doris Kearns. *Team of Rivals: The Political Genius of Abraham Lincoln*. New York: Simon and Schuster, 2005.

Grimsley, Elizabeth Todd. "Six Months at the White House." Originally written in 1895. *Journal of the Illinois State Historical Society* 19 (October 1926–January 1927): 43–73.

Helm, Katherine. *The True Story of Mary, Wife of Lincoln*. New York: Harper and Brothers, 1928.

Hicks, Thomas. "Lincoln's Portrait." In *Reminiscences of Abraham Lincoln by Distinguished Men of His Time*, edited by Allen Thorndike Rice, 593–607. New York: North American Publishing, 1886.

Holzer, Harold. *Abraham Lincoln. Mary Todd Lincoln* (monograph). Richmond, VA: United States Historical Society, 1984.

———, ed. *Dear Mr. Lincoln: Letters to the President*. New York: Addison Wesley, 1993.

———. *Lincoln at Cooper Union: The Speech That Made Abraham Lincoln President*. New York: Simon and Schuster, 2004; Simon and Schuster Lincoln Library paperback, 2006.

———, ed. *The Lincoln Mailbag: America Writes to the President, 1861–1865*. Carbondale: Southern Illinois University Press, 1998.

———. *Lincoln President-Elect: Abraham Lincoln and the Great Secession Winter 1860–1861*. New York: Simon and Schuster, 2008.

BIBLIOGRAPHY

Keckl[e]y, Elizabeth. *Behind the Scenes, or Thirty Years a Slave and Four Years in the White House.* New York: G. W. Carleton and Co., 1868.

Kunhardt, Dorothy Meserve, and Philip B. Kunhardt, Jr. *Twenty Days.* New York: Harper and Row, 1965.

Lockwood, John. "Toy Store Brightens Lincoln's Dark Days." *Washington Times*, December 20, 2003.

Lorant, Stefan. *Lincoln: A Picture Story of His Life.* Rev. ed. New York: W. W. Norton, 1969.

Miers, Earl Schenck, ed. *Lincoln Day by Day: A Chronology, 1809–1865.* 3 vols. Washington, DC: Lincoln Sesquicentennial Commission, 1960.

Neely, Mark E., and Harold Holzer. *The Lincoln Family Album.* Rev. ed. Carbondale: Southern Illinois University Press, 2006.

Nicolay, Helen. *Lincoln's Secretary: A Biography of John G. Nicolay.* New York: Longmans, Green, 1949.

Ostendorf, Lloyd. *Lincoln's Photographs: A Complete Album.* Rev. ed. Dayton, OH: Rockywood Press, 1998. Originally published as *Lincoln in Photographs*, co-written with Charles Hamilton, 1963.

Pfanz, Donald C. *The Petersburg Campaign: Abraham Lincoln at City Point, March 20–April 9, 1865.* Lynchburg, VA: H. E. Howard, 1989.

Pinsker, Matthew. *Lincoln's Sanctuary: Abraham Lincoln and the Soldiers' Home.* New York: Oxford University Press, 2003.

Pitch, Anthony S. *They Have Killed Papa Dead: The Road to Ford's Theatre, Abraham Lincoln's Murder, and the Rage for Vengeance.* Hanover, NH: Steerforth Press, 2009.

Randall, Ruth Painter. *Lincoln's Sons.* Boston: Little, Brown, 1955.

Sandburg, Carl. *Mary Lincoln, Wife and Widow.* New York: Harcourt, Brace, 1932.

Seward, Frances A. *Diary.* Seward Papers, University of Rochester.

Steers, Edward, Jr. *Blood on the Moon: The Assassination of Abraham Lincoln.* Lexington: University Press of Kentucky, 2001.

BIBLIOGRAPHY

Stoddard, William O. *Abraham Lincoln: The True Story of a Great Life*. New York: Fords, Howard, and Hulbert, 1884.

Stoddard, William O., and Michael Burlingame, eds. *Inside the White House in War Times: Memoirs and Reports of Lincoln's Secretary*. Lincoln: University of Nebraska Press, 2000. Originally published in 1890.

Symonds, Craig L. *Lincoln and His Admirals*. New York: Oxford University Press, 2008.

Temple, Wayne C. *Lincoln's Travels on the* River Queen *during the Last Days of His Life*. Mahomet, IL: Mayhaven Publishing, 2007.

———, ed. "Sketch of 'Tad' Lincoln." *Lincoln Herald* 60 (Fall 1958): 79–80.

Turner, Justin G., and Linda Levitt Turner. *Mary Todd Lincoln: Her Life and Letters*. New York: Alfred A. Knopf, 1972.

Warren, Louis A. *Lincoln's Youth: Indiana Years, Seven to Twenty-One, 1816–1830*. Indianapolis: Indiana Historical Society, 1991.

Wead, Doug. *All the President's Children: Triumph and Tragedy in the Lives of America's First Families*. New York: Atria Books, 2003.

Welles, Gideon. *The Diary of Gideon Welles*. 3 vols. Boston: Houghton Mifflin, 1911.

Whitney, Henry C. *Life on the Circuit with Lincoln*. Boston: Estes and Lauriat, 1892.

Wilson, Douglas L., and Rodney O. Davis, eds. *Herndon's Informants: Letters, Interviews, and Statements about Abraham Lincoln*. Urbana: University of Illinois Press, 1998.

Wilson, Rufus Rockwell. *Intimate Memories of Lincoln*. Elmira, NY: Primavera Press, 1945. (See especially Robert Lincoln's letter to Josiah G. Holland, June 6, 1865, pp. 498–499.)

———. *Lincoln Among His Friends*. Caldwell, ID: Caxton Printers, 1942. (See especially recollection by Fred Dubois, originally published in the *New York Times*, February 12, 1927.)

Notes

The source of each quotation in this book is found below. The citation indicates the first words of the quotation and its document source (using the following abbreviations or the author's last name). Most of the sources are listed in the bibliography. Complete citations are provided for those books not in the bibliography.

The following abbreviations are used:

BAK (Jean H. Baker, *Mary Todd Lincoln*)
CW (Roy P. Basler, ed., *The Collected Works of Abraham Lincoln*, 9 vols.)
F & F (Fehrenbacher and Fehrenbacher, *Recollected Words of Abraham Lincoln*)
FBC (Francis B. Carpenter, *Six Months at the White House with Abraham Lincoln: The Story of a Picture*)
HH (Harold Holzer, *Abraham Lincoln. Mary Todd Lincoln*)
HI (Wilson and Davis, eds., *Herndon's Informants*)
LFA (Neely and Holzer, *The Lincoln Family Album*)
LOR (Stefan Lorant, *Lincoln: A Picture Story of His Life*)
MTL (Turner and Turner, *Mary Todd Lincoln: Her Life and Letters*)
NIC (Helen Nicolay, *Lincoln's Secretary*)
PE (Harold Holzer, *Lincoln President-Elect*)

EPIGRAPH Page 5
"I regret…": CW, 4:129.

INTRODUCTION Page 8
"a grave boy" and "He had much…": LFA, p. 145.
"a large strong…": quoted in *New York Times*, "Young Abraham Lincoln," 1890, p. 3.

CHAPTER ONE Page 14
"a paradise in miniature," quoted in *Ohio Editor*, 1839.
"busy wilderness,": BAK, p. 76.
"a great deal of flourishing…": CW, 1:78.
"I am quite…": BAK, p. 76.
"I have been…": Ibid.
"and should not…": CW, 1:78.
"by littles": NIC, chapter 1.
"Prepare to die…": HH.
"could make a…": Gary, Ralph. *Following in Lincoln's Footsteps: A Historical Reference to Hundreds of Sites Visited by Abraham Lincoln*. New York: Carroll and Graf, 2001, p. 120.

"the very creature…": BAK, p. 85.
"herself more than when…": Randall, Ruth Painter. *The Courtship of Mr. Lincoln*. Boston: Little, Brown, 1957.
"Miss Todd, I want…": Ibid.
"he surely did!": Ibid.
"a very little…": Helm, p. 140.
"her head thrown…": Ibid.
"in origin…": Herndon, William H., and Jesse W. Weik. *Herndon's Life of Lincoln*. New York: Da Capo Press, 1942, p. 345.
"an understanding": Winkle, Kenneth J. *The Young Eagle: The Rise of Abraham Lincoln*. Dallas: Taylor Trade Publishing, 2001, pp. 186–87.
"We were engaged…": Ibid.
"Fatal First": BAK, p. 90.
"I am so poor…": CW, 3:400.
"It is bad to be…": Ibid.
"I am now the…": LOR, p. 48.
"Lincoln went crazy…": Ibid.
"his reach": Ibid.
"the never-absent…": Nicolay, John G., and John M. Hay. *Abraham Lincoln: A History*. New York: The Century Co., 1890. 10 volumes. Vol. 1, p. 94.
"emaciated in appearance": HH, p. 20.
"scarcely strong enough…": Ibid.
"No more will…": Angle, p. 96.
"to greet his…": Ibid.
"deems me unworthy…": BAK, p. 91.
"Richard should be…": Ibid.
"My old Father used…": CW, 1:280.
"the most pleasant one…": Ibid.
"You have now…": CW, 1:303.
"as pale and…": Herndon, William H., et. al. *Herndon's Life of Lincoln*. Lincoln Studies Center, Abraham Lincoln Bicentennial Commission, 2009, p. 144.
"Nothing new here": CW, 1:305.
"except my marrying…": Ibid.
"a namesake at…": CW, 1:319.
"We are but two…": CW, 1:328.

CHAPTER TWO Page 24
"a nice home-loving…": MTL, pp. 60, 506.
"We are not keeping…": CW, 1:325.
"first squall": F & F, p. 176.
"I'm glad it is…": F & F, p. 164.
"pretty much of…": CW, 1:325.
"Mrs. Lincoln had no…": BAK, p. 103.
"I was very…": Epstein, p. 81.
"I have often…": Goff, p. 8.

Notes

"thoroughly loved his wife": Whitney, p. 97.

"good husband": Ibid., p. 98.

"We have another…": CW, 1:391.

"Bobbie's lost! Bobbie's lost!": Randall, Ruth Painter. *Mary Lincoln: Biography of a Marriage*. Boston: Little, Brown, 1953, p. 118.

"Bob is…": CW, 1:391.

"I followed…": Goff, p. 13.

"There were two…": *Journal of the Illinois State Historical Society*, vol. 19, Oct.–Jan. 1926–27, p. 57.

"Good Lord, there…": Helm, p. 102.

CHAPTER THREE Page 34

"a bright boy": Goff, p. 14.

"seemed to have his own way": Ibid.

"a pleasant room…": BAK, p. 137.

"father has gone…": Angle, Paul. *The Living Lincoln: The Man and His Times, in His Own Words*. Barnes and Noble, 1992, p. 115.

"In this troublesome…": CW, 1:465.

"All the house…": Donald, David Herbert. *Lincoln*. New York: Simon and Schuster, 1995, p. 121.

"Eddy's dear little feet": Ibid., p. 130.

"I did not get rid of…": CW, 1:466.

"What did he…": Ibid.

"Do not fear the…": Epstein, p. 140.

"Even E[ddy's]…": Ibid.

"a little spell of sickness": Ibid., p. 139.

"*our* babies are asleep": Ibid., p. 140.

"triumphantly": Ibid., p. 139.

"*your hobby*": Ibid.

"*tenderness* broke forth": Ibid.

"fed it with bread himself": Ibid.

"delightful": Ibid.

"in the midst…": Ibid.

"throw it…": Ibid.

"Ed screaming &…": Ibid.

"*she* never appeared…": Ibid.

"Come on just…": CW, 1:478.

"I want to see you…": Ibid.

"a girl": CW, 1:496.

"Father expected to…": Ibid.

"but let it…": Ibid.

"hard to beat": Miers, 1:320.

"remarkably well": Ibid., p. 322.

"Mr. L. is not at home": MTL, p. 51.

"This makes the…": Ibid.

CHAPTER FOUR Page 42

"We Miss…": Angle, *The Living Lincoln*, p. 143.

"He looked at…": Epstein, p. 160.

"Eat, Mary…": BAK, p. 126.

"I suppose you…": Angle, *The Living Lincoln*, p. 143.

"Little Eddie": *Illinois State Journal* (AL Bicentennial Commission Web site, www.lincolnbicentennial.gov—see "Edward Baker Lincoln").

"crimson tinge…": Ibid.

"our second boy…": BAK, p. 128.

"I grieve to…": Ibid.

"we wept together…": Bayne, p. 14.

CHAPTER FIVE Page 48

"scampered about on…": Helm, p. 103.

"'This rock shall…'": Ibid., p. 108.

"'brave knights…'": Ibid.

"was nicknamed…": MTL, p. 284.

"sick abed": CW, 2:97.

"baby-sickness": Ibid.

"more painful…": Ibid.

"Perhaps you know…": MTL, p. 465.

"the mother of three…": Epstein, p. 213.

"our *dear little Taddie*": Ibid., p. 221.

"cockeye": Goff, p. 17.

"delighted in…": Clinton, Catherine. *Mrs. Lincoln: A Life*. New York: HarperCollins, 2009, p. 89.

"Mrs L got the…": HI, p. 453.

"Lincoln…would pick up…": Ibid.

"Bobbie will die!": Goff, p. 10.

"Well, Judge, I…": Ibid., p. 18.

"pretending to be…": Helm, p. 113.

"did not realize…": Ibid.

"his long legs taking…": Ibid.

"Mrs. L would whip…": HI, p. 597.

"permissive": Goff, p. 11.

"Spare the rod…": Ibid.

"Spare the rod": Ibid.

"spare the rod": Wilson, *Lincoln Among His Friends*, p. 99.

"boisterous": Ibid.

"the most loving…": MTL, p. 66.

"He gave us all…": HI, p. 357.

"It is my pleasure…": F & F, p. 296.

"little devils": Angle, Paul M. *The Lincoln Reader*. New Brunswick, NJ: Rutgers University Press, 1947, p. 190.

"They soon gutted…": Ibid.

"gutted the shelves…": Ibid.

Notes

"had they shat…": LFA, p. 46.
"I have felt…": Goff, p. 12.
"He worshipped…": LFA, p. 46.
"would take his…": HI, p. 453.
"[H]e never made…": Goff, p. 13.
"the very best…": HI, p. 485.
"He was a…": Ibid.
"Why, Mr. Lincoln": Randall, p. 41.
"put down that…": Ibid.
"it's a big thing…": Ibid., pp. 42–43.
"to make things…": Ibid.
"I can't…": Ibid.
"'cause I ate…": Ibid.
"trot out Bob…": Angle, *The Lincoln Reader*, p. 190.
"on fire": Holzer, Harold, ed. *The Lincoln-Douglas Debates: The First Complete Unexpurgated Text.* New York: HarperCollins, 1993, p. 1.

CHAPTER SIX Page 60
"A house divided…": CW, 2:461.
"half *slave* and half *free*": Ibid.
"It will become *all* one thing": Ibid.
"or all the other": Ibid.
"While I was a boy…": LFA, p. 26.
"a new process…": Ibid.
"like his mother…": Ibid.
"If you are going…": Epstein, p. 221.
"This town is a…": Holzer, Harold, ed. *Lincoln As I Knew Him: Gossip, Tributes & Revelations from His Best Friends and Worst Enemies.* Chapel Hill, NC: Algonquin, 1999, p. 28.
"*Words* cannot…": MTL, p. 58.
"we did just…": Epstein, p. 205.
"I am feeling quite…": MTL, p. 58.
"at times I…": Ibid., p. 64.
"I miss Bob…": Ibid., p. 59.
"Just what's the…": F & F, p. 141.
"I've got three…": Ibid.

CHAPTER SEVEN Page 66
"the speech that…": Holzer, *Lincoln at Cooper Union*, p. 226.
"a neat-looking…": LFA, p. 27.
"Let us have…" and "that right…": Holzer, *Lincoln at Cooper Union*, p. 175.
"made me President": Holzer, *Lincoln at Cooper Union*, p. 100.
"Will you speak…": Ibid., p. 183.
"to see how…": Ibid., p. 312n10.
"I have scarcely…": CW, 4:87.

"He displays…": Holzer, *Lincoln at Cooper Union*, p. 185.
"persuaded to deliver…": Ibid., p. 186.
"he will answer…": Ibid.
"What a darned fool…": Ibid., p. 187.
"very good dresser": Ibid.
"succeeded in arranging…": Ibid.
"We sat and…": Ibid.
"untangled those long legs": Ibid.
"not ten minutes…": Ibid.
"Dear Wife…": Ibid., p. 190.
"I would that…" Ibid. (paperback edition), p. 20.
"Cluskey plays the…": Ibid., p. 191.
"Robert, you ought…": Ibid.
"urgent to have": MTL, p. 64.
"This summer…": Ibid., p. 66.
"somewhat pleasanter…": F & F, p. 255.
"noiselessly into the…": Rice, Allen Thorndike, ed. *Reminiscences of Abraham Lincoln by Distinguished Men of His Time.* New York: North American Publishing, 1886, pp. 598–99.
"The brightest blue": Ibid.
"smeared that in…": Ibid.
"I saw their…": Ibid.
"as still as…": Ibid.
"the mildest tone…": Ibid.
"the little fellows…": Ibid.
"everywhere at once…": Randall, p. 74.
"Come here…": Ibid.
"Did you hear…": Wilson, *Intimate Memories of Lincoln*, p. 316.
"He got that…": Ibid.
"with what interested…": Randall, p. 74.
"about the room": Ibid.
"Our eldest boy, Bob…": CW, 4:81–82.
"having a little season…": F & F, p. 35.
"I scarcely know…": MTL, p. 68.

CHAPTER EIGHT Page 80
"juvenile yells": PE, p. 91.
"Is that the old woman?": Ibid.
"I have got…": CW, 4:130.
"would look a…": Ibid.
"Have you any…": Ibid.
"My dear little Miss": Ibid., p. 129.
"making the house…": PE, p. 189.
"back at Exeter" and "very much at home": Donald, *Lincoln*, p. 76.
"Aint you beginning…": Randall, pp. 82–83.
"a fellow…": Ibid.

Notes

"must be the…": Ibid.

"a vast sea…": Ibid.

"it must have been…": PE, p. 161.

"to please…": Ibid., p. 198.

"The Old Lady…": Ibid., p. 199.

"the improving influences…": Ibid., p. 200.

"heir apparent": Ibid.

"bringing up the…": Ibid.

"a striking contrast…": Ibid.

"a young man of…much dignity" and "a dutiful and affectionate son": LFA (original edition), p. 66.

"cockeye": Goff, p. 17.

"winter of secession,": PE, p. 192.

"hundreds of well…": Ibid., p. 285.

"Good evening…": Ibid., p. 286.

"his father gave…": Ibid.

"During my childhood…": Robert T. Lincoln to Josiah Holland, Abraham Lincoln Papers, Library of Congress, June 6, 1865.

"gilded prison": PE, p. 200.

CHAPTER NINE Page 94

"My friends…": CW, 4:190.

"look of stupefaction": Wilson, Douglas L. *Lincoln's Sword: The Presidency and the Power of Words*. New York: Alfred A. Knopf, 2007, p. 305n.

"Now, you keep it!": NIC, p. 65.

"The old man…": PE, p. 311.

"probably the happiest…": NIC, pp. 63–64.

"carefree": Ibid.

"Do you want to…": PE, p. 315.

"Mrs. L. behaves…": Ibid., p. 332.

"Where are the…": Ibid., p. 353.

"Have you any more?": Ibid.

"to bring a tough…": Ibid.

"the more he…": Ibid.

"I wish they wouldn't…": Randall, p. 92.

"plenty of bears": PE, p. 364.

"guest star": Ibid., p. 575n.

"It ain't best…": F & F, p. 494.

"pale and very…": PE, p. 451.

"the better angels of our nature": CW, 4:271.

"We must not be enemies": Ibid.

"Though passion…": Ibid.

"peace" and "a sword?": Ibid., p. 261.

CHAPTER TEN Page 112

"sick of Washington…" and "to get back to his college": Randall, p. 92.

"never unpacked his…": LFA, p. 2.

"I scarcely even…": Ibid., p. 66.

"shabby": Ibid., p. 64.

"better than any house…": Donald, *Lincoln*, p. 313.

"came and went…": LFA, p. 50.

"Tad and Willie Lincoln have…": Stoddard, p. 50.

"and they are the happy…": Ibid.

"a peculiarly promising boy": LFA, p. 50.

"Gentlemen—I am very happy…": Diary of Fanny Seward, February 5, 1863.

"full of merry mischief…": LFA, p. 50.

"interpreter": Ibid., p. 67.

"I enclose you…": Randall, p. 121.

"There was no…": Ibid.

"a remarkably bright…": Anonymous, "The President's Son." *American Phrenological Journal*; APS online, p. 77.

"I know every step…": Donald, *Lincoln*, p. 159.

"different from most…": Diary of Fanny Seward, April 11, 1862.

"Oh, mother, I…": Ibid.

"the hope": Randall, p. 227.

"old age": Ibid.

"merry sunshine": MTL, p. 189.

"We have only…": LFA (original edition), p. 23.

"Willie was the most…": Bayne, p. 8.

"Let the children…": Ibid., p. 47.

"livelier": Ibid., p. 14.

"Well, Tad" and "I suppose it's…": Ibid.

"But they got away…": Ibid., p. 48.

"Oh, yes, they…": Ibid.

"Julie, come quick…": Ibid.

"You're not fit…": Ibid., p. 56.

"and I ought…": Ibid.

"Think you had…": CW, 6:256.

"with great pride" and "Hurrah for Abe Lincoln!": LFA, p. 68.

"clinging to the saddle…": Brooks, Noah. "A Boy in the White House." *St. Nicholas Magazine*, vol. 10, Nov. 1882–May 1883 (part 1), p. 57.

"The Doll Jack is pardoned…": Bayne, p. 59.

"make my hair grow": Ibid., p. 44.

"loved Tad's cats…": HI, p. 466.

"It interests the boy" and "and does them…": F & F, p. 415.

"He had a very…": Burlingame, Michael, ed. *At Lincoln's Side: John Hay's Civil War Correspondence and Selected Writings*. Carbondale: Southern Illinois University, 2000, pp. 111–12.

Notes

"kept the house…": Nicolay, Helen. *The Boys' Life of Abraham Lincoln.* New York: The Century Company, 1906, p. 72.

"Tad, why did…": Kunhardt, p. 76.

"both or either…": LFA (original edition), p. 67.

"when grave statesmen…": Ibid.

"were of more…": Ibid.

CHAPTER ELEVEN Page 126

"the idolized one": MTL, p. 128.

"up-to-date" and "the ghosts…": Kunhardt, p. 111.

"If I go he…": Bayne, p. 82.

"Well, Nicolay, my…": Donald, *Lincoln*, p. 336.

"the *deep waters*": LFA, p. 62.

"family affliction": French, p. 388.

"buried his face…": Keckl[e]y, p. 101.

"My poor boy" and "he was too…": Clinton, *Mrs. Lincoln: A Life*, p. 167.

"He was fonder…": Stoddard, p. 66.

"Dear Willie" and "He was pure gold": Bayne, p. 70.

"all of his boyish frolic" and "a child of great…": LFA, p. 61.

"kept about his…" and "gave no…": Wilson, *Intimate Memories of Lincoln*, p. 400.

"Your son is alive…" and "Alive! Alive!" and "Surely you mock me": Kunhardt, p. 137.

"Grief fills the room…": Shakespeare, William. *The Life and Death of King John.*

"Did you ever dream…": F & F, p. 78.

"Do you ever find…" and "Ever since Willie's…": Birnes, William J., and Joel Martin. *The Haunting of America: From the Salem Witch Trials to Harry Houdini.* New York: Forge Books, 2009, p. 201.

"We have met…": MTL, p. 127.

"I can scarcely…": Ibid.

"how the heart bleeds" and "our precious…": Ibid., p. 147.

"crushing bereavement" and "sainted boy": Ibid., p. 127.

"fiery furnace of affliction": Ibid., p. 189.

"It makes me…": BAK, p. 213.

"Mother" and "do you see that…": Keckl[e]y, pp. 102–03.

"tossing with typhoid": Goodwin, p. 420.

"I hope you will pray" and "and, if it…": F & F, p. 362.

"This is the hardest…": Goodwin, p. 420.

"I had become…": MTL, p. 189.

"interfered" and "to put a stop…": BAK, p. 215.

"very beautiful" and "the grounds around…" and "the idolized one…": MTL, p. 128.

"When I think over…": Ibid.

"God, can *alone*…": Ibid., p. 627.

"very near" and "a very slight veil" and "the 'loved…'": Ibid., p. 256.

"He comes to me…": Helm, p. 227.

"If Willie did not come…": Ibid., p. 217.

"Dear little Taddie…" and "bears up…": MTL, p. 128.

"but when Tad came in…" and "he threw himself…": Bayne, p. 83.

"You must excuse him, Julia" and "You know what he remembers": Ibid.

CHAPTER TWELVE Page 138

"little troublesome sunshine": MTL, p. 425.

"It is, *sometimes*…" and "to be a favorite…": MTL, pp. 149–50.

"I don't care…": HI, p. 445.

"Mr. L. told…": Ibid.

"I guess I must…": F & F, p. 415.

"You shall not…": Ibid.

"that in my life…" and "never required…": MTL, p. 251.

"Let him run" and "There's time enough…": F & F, p. 57.

"thought very little" and "of any tutor…": LFA, p. 92.

"power of taming…": Ibid.

"special gift": Ibid.

"Most boys, by nature…": Crook, p. 24.

"He's a good turkey…": Burlingame, *Lincoln Observed*, pp. 198–99.

"infant goblin…": Burlingame, Michael. *At Lincoln's Side*, pp. 111–12.

"tricksy little sprite" and "that sad and solemn…" LFA, p. 52.

"the only…": Ibid., p. 69.

"plots and commotions" and "the absolute…": Burlingame, *At Lincoln's Side*, pp. 111–12.

"He was so…": Ibid.

"was a merry, warm-blooded…": Wilson, *Intimate Memories of Lincoln*, p. 400.

"took infinite comfort…": Burlingame, *At Lincoln's Side*, pp. 111–12.

"would perch upon…": Wilson, *Intimate Memories of Lincoln*, p. 400.

"Now I wonder…": Bullard, p. 9.

"He can't keep…": Kunhardt, p. 137.

"would pick him…": Wilson, *Intimate Memories of Lincoln*, p. 400.

"a rather grotesque-looking…": Temple, Wayne C. "Sketch of 'Tad' Lincoln," p. 80.

Notes

"see the people": Kunhardt, p. 76.

"I want to give…": "The Signal Flag." The Brandywine Valley Civil War Round Table, December 2006.

"had no business" and "very mildly" and "Tad, go…": Carpenter, *Six Months at the White House with Abraham Lincoln*, p. 293.

"Has not the boy…" and "bent on punishment": Ibid.

"There" and "go ahead, it is all right now": FBC, p. 92.

"Tad is a peculiar child…": Ibid.

"The President never…" and "than when, stealing…": Ibid., p. 93.

"some of the idlest…": Holzer, *The Lincoln Mailbag*, p. 42.

"admonished for smoking in Harvard Square" and "impress upon" and "decorum": Holzer, *Dear Mr. Lincoln*, pp. 314–15.

"Son, what are you going…" and "If you do" and "you should learn…" and "That is the only…": F & F, p. 298.

"Tad was in bitter…" and "his heaviest grief…": Burlingame, *With Lincoln*, p. 126.

"a dead loss": FBC, p. 45.

"the fun of the thing": Carpenter, *Six Months at the White House with Abraham Lincoln*, p. 300.

"I found it out an hour ago" and "and thinking it…" and "instead of punishing…": FBC, p. 300.

"Tad, if you will…" and " as noisy as early" and "Father, I want my dollar": Ibid., p. 94.

"Tad, do you think you have earned it?": Ibid.

"Well, my son…": Ibid.

"If Tad lives to be…" and "he will be what…": Kunhardt, p. 76.

CHAPTER THIRTEEN Page 150

"charming place" and "we can be as…": LFA, p. 81.

"a great favorite": Pinsker, p. 78.

"boy was here…": Ibid.

"Guards and…": Ibid., p. 80.

"Dear little Taddie…": MTL, pp. 139–40.

"[W]e can not escape history" and "In *giving* freedom…": CW, 5:37.

"ragged & dirty": Pinsker, p. 143.

"my notions of…": Keckl[e]y, p. 42.

"I have not got my cat": Pinsker, p. 93.

"I do not think…": CW, 6:283.

"very slightly hurt" and "uneasy": Ibid., p. 314.

"Come to Washington": Ibid., p. 323.

"Why do I hear…": CW, 6:327.

"in tears" and "with his head…": Goff, p. 52.

"Tell dear Tad…": CW, 6:371–72.

"Tell Taddy that…": Holzer, *Dear Mr. Lincoln*, p. 321.

"The air is so clear…" and "Nothing very particular…": CW, 6:471.

"The Dr has just left…": MTL, p. 158.

The Gettysburg Address: CW, 7:23.

"Tad says are the goats well?": Holzer, *Dear Mr. Lincoln*, p. 327.

"Tell Tad the…": Ibid.

"He does everything very well…": Goff, p. 59.

"Now that we…" and "Poor Mr. Lincoln…": Keckl[e]y, p. 53.

CHAPTER FOURTEEN Page 168

"the serpents" and "crossed our pathways": MTL, p. 200.

"I know that…": Helm, p. 227.

"Many a poor mother…": Ibid.

"Don't I know…" and "Before this war is ended" and "I may be…": Ibid., p. 228.

"wishes to see something…" and "I do not wish…": CW, 8:223.

"Could he, without…" and "with some…": Ibid.

"most happy to have him": Holzer, *The Lincoln Mailbag*, p. 213.

"With malice toward…": CW, 8:333.

"Now bring your father…": Ostendorf, p. 213.

"Taddie very much": MTL, p. 2311.

"well & in good spirits": Basler, Roy P., ed. *Collected Works of Abraham Lincoln: Supplement*. Westport, CT: Greenwood Press, 1974, p. 285.

"Tad and I are both well" and "and will be glad…": CW, 8:384.

"Bless the Lord…" and "Don't kneel to me…" and "tumbling and shouting…": Goodwin, p. 719.

"Master Tad Lincoln…": CW, 8:393.

"Tad was so excited…" and "with a great shout of applause" and "the young hopeful…": Burlingame, *Lincoln Observed*, p. 182.

"uproarious cheers" and "was lugged back…": Ibid.

"fairly captured" and "lawful prize": CW, 8:393.

"Tad wants some…" and "Let Master Tad…": Ibid., p. 395.

"very intelligent" and "those who serve our cause as soldiers": Ibid., p. 403.

"That is the last speech…": Steers, p. 91.

"Come, give me another!": Randall, p. 161.

"What shall we…" and "No, no…": LOR, p. 258.

Notes

"It is a good face…": F & F, p. 275.
"We must both…" and "[B]etween the…": MTL, p. 285.
"The pleasure…": Randall, p. 145.
"his terrible grief": *The Century Illustrated Monthly Magazine*, vol. 45, p. 635.
"speak to him…": Randall, p. 163.
"O Tom Pen…": Pitch, p. 141.
"Why didn't he…": Kauffman, Michael W. *American Brutus: John Wilkes Booth and the Lincoln Conspiracies.* New York: Random House, 2005, p. 38.
"Mother, please put…": Goff, p. 70.
"weeping and wailing…": Welles, 2:290.
"Oh, Mr. Welles…": Ibid.
"Pa is dead…" and "I am only Tad…": Keckl[e]y, pp. 195–96.

CHAPTER FIFTEEN Page 186
"Don't cry…": Keckl[e]y, p. 190.
"terrible outbursts" and "Don't cry…": Ibid., p. 195.
"as if his heart…": Pitch, p. 227.
"God bless…": Sheet music in the Abraham Lincoln Presidential Library, Springfield, IL.
"My heart…" and "he seemed…": Randall, p. 169.
"Bidding Adieu…": MTL, p. 268.
"Alas, all is…": BAK, p. 254.
"of their counsellor…": MTL, p. 242.
"humiliated": Ibid., p. 274.
"Living Monuments…": Ibid., p. 315.
"lovely nature" and "in our day…": Ibid., p. 250.
"In all my plans…": Lachman, Charles. *The Last Lincolns: The Rise and Fall of a Great American Family.* New York: Sterling Publishing, 2008, p. 59.
"almost as soon be dead" and "dreary" and "revolting": BAK, p. 257.
"even for a day" and "Taddie is going…": LFA, p. 16.
"After all…few children…": MTL, p. 273.
"Taddie is learning…": Ibid., p. 284.
"happy family": Carpenter, "Anecdotes and Reminiscences of President Lincoln," p. 763.
"prized": MTL, p. 279.
"was a very…": LFA, p. 87.
"There was never…": Randall, p. 249.
"met some fine…" and "very happy": MTL, p. 481.
"marriage passed off…" and "very rich": Ibid., p. 484.
"a great deal of trouble in the future": Helm.
"care" and "widow of a…": MTL, p. 493.
"precious child Taddie": BAK, p. 289.

"So, is he…": LFA, p. 104.
"[I]t appears to…": Ibid., p. 122.
"grandmamma" and "too much…": Ibid.
"Tad is almost…": Randall, p. 207.
"beautiful, darling…": BAK, pp. 305–06.
"modest and cordial": Burlingame, *At Lincoln's Side*, p. 111.
"His mother" and "in great affliction": BAK, p. 308.
"There is no…": Clinton, *Mrs. Lincoln: A Life*, p. 291.
"As grievous…": BAK, p. 309.
"My idolized &…": MTL, p. 596.
"Mother, if you…": LFA, p. xvi-xvii.
"Oh, Robert…": BAK, p. 325.
"Robert T. Lincoln" and "Do not fail…": MTL, pp. 615–16.
"Two prominent…": BAK, p. 349.
"God, can *alone*…": MTL, p. 627.
"But waiting" and "is so long": Ibid., p. 630.
"wretched young man": Ibid., p. 631.
"good" and "a monster…": Berry, p. 185.
"on account…": Emerson, p. 163.
"I have been…": MTL, p. 682.
"Among the passengers…": Ibid., p. 704.
"very feeble…": Ibid., p. 711.
"grace": LFA, p. 123.
"morbid" and "It seems…": Ibid., p. 18.
"the hardest of many…": Goff, p. 196.
"I did not…": Ibid.

EPILOGUE Page 204
"just out of…": Tarbell, Ida M. *All in the Day's Work: An Autobiography.* Urbana: University of Illinois Press, 2003, p. 166.
"in the shadow…" and "on his own…": Goff, p. 262.
"I'm as far…": LFA, p. 22.

Index

Pages numbers in **boldface** refer to photographs and/or captions.

Index

Index

Index

Index

Index

Index

Index

Picture Credits

Abraham Lincoln Presidential Library & Museum (ALPLM): 8 (bottom right), 10, 16, 24, 28, 29 (right), 46, 48, 51, 89, 93, 165, 171, 209 (right).

From the "Collection of Keya Morgan, Lincolnimages.com": 29 (left).

College of Psychic Studies, London: 199.

"Donald L. Carrick, The White House Historical Association": 1802: 163.

Ford's Theatre National Historic Site: 152.

Harold Holzer: 27, 53, 59, 66, 82, 85, 106, 107, 125, 154 (bottom right), 174 (bottom right), 183, 192.

Illinois State Historical Library: 97.

Library of Congress, Prints and Photographs Division: LC-DIG-ppmsca-19305, Anthony Berger: front jacket and cover (large oval), 1; LC-USZ62-7992: back jacket and cover, 14; LC-USZ62-2279: 11; LC-USZ61-2039: 19; LC-USZ6-2094: 30; LC-USZ6-2095: 31; LC-USZ62-110213, John Plumbe: 34; LC-USZ62-5659: 40; LC-USZ62-36582: 42; LC-B2-3855-5: 52; LC-USZ62-60931-A: 64; LC-USZ62-5803: 68; LC-USZ62-15984: 84; LC-USZ62-10837: 90; LC-USZ62-11493: 91; LC-USZ61-216: 98; LC-USZ62-45872: 102; LC-USZ62-89615: 103; LC-USZ62-50817: 105; LC-USZ62-22734: 109; 111; LC-USZ62-90258: 115; LC-B8171-7850: 124; LC-USZ62-112729: 126; LC-DIG-pga-03266: 156; LC-USZ62-47037: 157; LC-USZ62-783: 167; LC-B8171-7765: 180: LC-USZ62-7542, Henry F. Warren: 230.

From the Lincoln Financial Foundation Collection, Courtesy of the Indiana State Museum: front jacket and cover (three small photos) and 60, 8 (top left), 13, 33, 69, 75, 77, 78, 80, 86, 94, 96, 110, 112, 119, 120, 122, 129, 134, 136, 137, 138, 146, 148, 150, 154 (top left), 155, 161, 162, 166, 168, 170, 172, 174 (top left), 176, 178, 182, 184, 186, 189, 190, 191, 196, 197, 204, 206, 207, 208, 209 (left).

Courtesy of the Mary Todd Lincoln House: 17.

Still Picture Branch of the National Archives and Records: 111-B-2088: 144.

The Western Reserve Historical Society, Cleveland, Ohio: 164.

Courtesy of The Wills House, Gettysburg: 159.

This is the last photograph of Abraham Lincoln. It was made on March 6, 1865, two days after his inauguration for a second term as president and only six weeks before his murder. It is said that Lincoln's son Tad asked his father to pose for the cameraman, Henry Warren, who earlier had taken a picture of the little boy on his horse. At Tad's request, Lincoln walked outside onto the White House balcony, where he squinted into the March sun for this final pose.

ACKNOWLEDGMENTS

For their many years of help and advice on this project, the author would like to thank Dr. Brad Hoch of the Wills House in Gettysburg; Cindy VanHorn, who so expertly manages the former Lincoln Museum image collection for its new home at the Indiana State Museum; Seth Bongartz of Hildene, Robert T. Lincoln's home in Manchester, Vermont; Harry Rubenstein at the Smithsonian's National Museum of American History in Washington, D.C.; Paul Tetrault, producing director at Ford's Theatre in Washington, as well as James Cornelius and the entire staff; Illinois State Historian Thomas F. Schwartz and his able colleagues at the Abraham Lincoln Presidential Library and Museum in Springfield; and Tim Townsend at Springfield's Lincoln Home. All have been most generous with pictures, documents, details, and counsel.

The recent literature on the Lincoln marriage and family has helped shed fresh light on these complex relationships, and in addition to pioneering authors Linda Levitt Turner and Jean H. Baker, the author is grateful to Catherine Clinton and Charles Lachman for their important new biographies of Mary and the "last Lincolns," respectively.

Twenty years ago, I had the pleasure of researching and co-writing *The Lincoln Family Album* with Mark E. Neely, Jr., a volume from which much information in this book originates. I gratefully acknowledge Professor Neely as well as the publisher of that volume, John Duff, then of Doubleday, and Sylvia Frank Rodrigue of Southern Illinois University Press, who brought out a new, improved, and updated paperback edition in 2006.

Many of the photographic images illustrating this book come from the original Lincoln family photo album, which was discovered by the late historian James T. Hickey. Mark Neely bought the collection for the Lincoln Museum in the 1980s, and his successor as director, Joan Flinspach, preserved and displayed the images until the collection was transferred to Indianapolis in 2009. Both deserve the thanks of readers of this book, and lovers of history everywhere, for their work in securing these precious relics for all time.

Finally—and above all—I am truly grateful to editor Carolyn P. Yoder, who commissioned and waited patiently for this book, and has expertly and lovingly guided it to publication.

—H.H.